HOW TO WRITE
Tools for the Craft

For Marianne, companion in this

HOW TO WRITE
Tools for the Craft

ROBERT MOHR

University College Dublin Press
Preas Choláiste Ollscoile Bhaile Átha Cliath

First published 1998 by University College Dublin Press,
Newman House, St Stephen's Green, Dublin 2, Ireland
Reprinted 2005

© Robert Mohr 1998

ISBN 1 900621 15 0

Cataloguing in Publication data available from the British Library

Typeset in 11/12 Bembo, 10/11 Times and Gill Sans
by Elaine Shiels, Bantry, Co. Cork, Ireland

Printed & Bound in Great Britain by MPG Books Ltd, Bodmin, Cornwall

Contents

Acknowledgements

I would like to thank those who have assisted in the making of this book: Professor William Robinson, mentor, for the original writing project; Kevin Hurley for the opportunity to restructure the course; Professor Declan Kiberd for seeing value in both the book and the course; Professor Tom Garvin for encouragement; Professor Jim Mays, Professor Stephen Mennell and Dr Vera Regan for their support; Barbara Mennell for her careful attention to detail and her gentle guidance; and my writing students for those hours of classroom refinement. My greatest debt extends to my wife, Marianne, who, knowing this material thoroughly, provided essential advice and materials for nearly every portion of the book.

'My Wood' by E.M. Forster is reproduced by permission of the Provost and Scholars of King's College, Cambridge, and the Society of Authors as the Literary Representative of the E.M. Forster Estate. 'Georgia O'Keeffe' is reproduced with the permission of Joan Didion. The extract from the essay on 'A Changing Society: Ireland since the 1960s' by Tom Boylan, Chris Curtin and Michael Laver, from *Irish Studies: A General Introduction* edited by Thomas Bartlett, Chris Curtin, Riana O'Dwyer and Gearóid Ó Tuathaigh is published by permission of Gill & Macmillan, Dublin, Ireland.

ROBERT MOHR
Dublin, May 1998

1. Introduction

Every proficient writer needs to master the same craft. This craft has its structures, its conventions (rules), and its techniques; a writer plies them in the same way that a master carpenter manipulates tools to make accurate cuts and joints, that a tailor deftly cuts and stitches, and that a financial planner skilfully arranges a portfolio. Without a good knowledge of the craft, a writer struggles with a fundamental handicap which keeps the writing from taking clear and graceful form, much as a weekend carpenter flounders with the tools and materials which a professional carpenter manipulates with obvious skill, much as an amateur investor poorly invests money. In this book I propose to lay out the fundamental structures and techniques of joining which all professional writers assume as the conventions of their craft, whether they write functionally, critically, or creatively; or whether they stay within those conventions or supersede them for expressive purposes.

I begin at the foundation of all writing structure by distinguishing the phrase and the clause. I proceed to define the core of a clause and demonstrate ways to set the core into proper focus within the sentence. I then present several writing structures, each of which has a specific grammatical function in the sentence, each of which has its own way of joining into the sentence fabric. These structures and their joinery must be learned not only because one wants to produce grammatically correct writing but also because a writer's thoughts actually begin to emerge already formed into these structures. At that point thinking becomes sharper, and clear writing comes more quickly. Then form and content merge.

For instance, since writers know that the subject and verb, the core of the sentence, are the most important structural parts, they automatically will put the word which *logically* names the subject of the writing into the *grammatical* subject position and then will search directly for the most accurate verb to tell what that subject does (see chapter 6, pp. 22–30). This is both a meaningful and a structural decision. After the foundation of a strong core is set down, all additions get attached properly to it. A verbal phrase, one of the structures we will consider, can show an action going on simultaneously beside the core action, and a practised writer will know how to join it correctly to the core. Or an adjective clause can easily add a whole block of information to a single noun within the sentence; it too has its joining technique. Once a writer masters each structure and its joining technique, no writing task is insurmountable. Rather, that writer will communicate the subtle complexity of any subject with control and grace.

The most important introductory point I shall make about the structure of writing defines a general principle of organisation. Succinctly put, this principle states: 'As in the sentence, so in the paragraph, so in the whole document'. If the three parts of this principle open out, they tell us this.

Every sentence has its core – a subject and a verb – to which every phrase and clause in the sentence is properly joined, attached either to the subject or to the verb or secondarily to something that is attached directly to the subject or verb. Nothing in the sentence can be left dangling, unattached; everything *must* be properly joined into the sentence fabric.

As every sentence has its core, so every paragraph has its main assertion, a topic sentence to which every other sentence in the paragraph is attached, either directly or indirectly through another sentence. Any sentence not joined deliberately into the body of the paragraph by a traceable link must be removed and replaced where it belongs or thrown onto the cutting floor. To clarify this point and to show how this cohesion in the paragraph can be accomplished, I will present three types of paragraph structures which professional writers produce: the coordinate sequence, the subordinate sequence and the mixed sequence paragraph. [1]

As every sentence has its core and every paragraph has its topic sentence, so too every extended piece of writing has its main controlling idea to which every topic sentence is linked. This controlling idea is expressed in the introduction through a thesis statement, or through the terms of reference, that definitive statement of subject-purpose-result in a report which makes an assertion that the body of the document promises to flesh out. Each topic sentence brings out an aspect of the general thesis statement and, therefore, is linked to it.

All books on writing offer very good advice on how to organise the writing task. Yet among them, it is difficult to find a systematic exposition of writing structures, a system of applied grammar which a person can learn and employ. I have found that most people's difficulty in writing comes not so much in lacking something to say or in not knowing how to acquire information or even how to put the information into an overall logical order, but in not knowing how consciously to compose precise sentences that a reader will read because they are clear. The problem extends back twenty to twenty-five years when the study of grammar was abandoned in formal education. Consequently, most people embark upon their careers having been denied an essential piece of knowledge. While this book is not a study of grammar, it applies grammatically based structures to the purpose of writing. For grammar-to-purpose revives the knowledge of writing structures and puts them back into the hands of people who need to compose well-crafted sentences, paragraphs, whole essays or reports.

Every written presentation is a body that has a brain (subject/topic), a heart (verb/thesis), and a circulatory flow (good joining/development): a living, cohesive body. Therefore, it makes sense to state in the general principle of organisation, that this body coheres similarly in the micro-structure – the sentence core plus its additions – as it does all the way through to the macro-structure: the introductory thesis statement plus its topic sentences. 'As in the sentence, so in the paragraph, so in the whole document.' The principle of organisation holds true throughout every level of writing. My purpose in leading the reader through each of the writing structures is to give a clear demonstration of how to compose any piece of writing based upon this cohesive organising principle (see figure 1).

Finally, once I have presented the structures, I offer a brief chapter on practical summary writing and a long chapter on report writing. Several organising procedures and schemes which I want to cover appear in the chapter on the report. It is, furthermore, both a demonstration of report layout, being set in reporting format, and a guide to constructing one.

The final introductory point I should like the reader to appreciate is spoken by Polonius in *Hamlet*. 'Since brevity is the soul of wit, I will be brief.' I have kept this book deliberately brief, almost skeletal, because I want it to be accessible, useful. It presents its information and moves on. No book can teach writing; writing is a skill in the hand, acquired only as one practises it, like any craft. I invite the reader to take structural information away from this book and ply it towards whatever writing task comes to hand. Practice is the only means to master the craft of writing.

Figure 1 This diagram of boxes within boxes portrays the overall organisation in writing and is based upon the general principle of organisation: as in the sentence, so in the paragraph, so in the whole document.

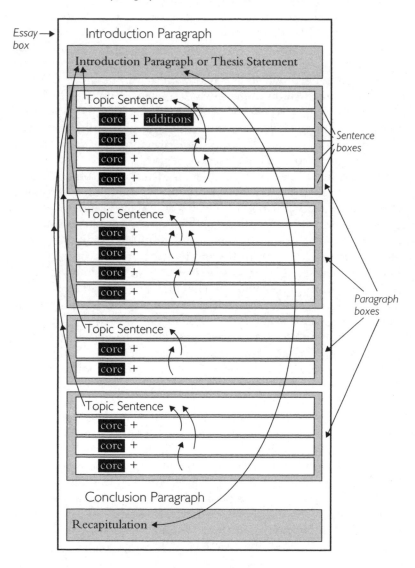

2. The Writing Process

First, no writer can begin to approach a writing task without two clear points. One point is a subject to write about, and the other point is a purpose that directs both the research and writing on that subject. As soon as possible you should write out a statement declaring your subject and your intention. This is your thesis statement, your terms of reference, your theme. Many writers pin this statement onto the wall in front of them and look at it frequently while writing. It helps keep them on track.

Next, you cannot write on a topic you have only vague and scattered information about. Therefore, research and reading are where writing starts. Once you start reading and gathering notes, writing begins to come out in rudimentary form. Keep these fragments as they may turn into paragraphs in time. Research and writing happen together. One does not finish research before attempting to write a sentence. There is a symbiotic relationship between research and writing. Writing sharpens the mind and directs it in research. And, of course, research spawns writing. As these sentences seem to travel in a circle, so do research and writing circle about one another.

Every time you have a moment of clarity amid your research, a moment when several threads of information or thought start to form a pattern you can perceive, and, in those moments, you begin to form statements in your mind, get to pen and paper as quickly as possible and write down what you are thinking. Do not censor the material. Simply write and save it for later. Over time you will gather disparate pieces of writing which will help you to break into more formal writing eventually. These scraps provide a remedy for writer's block as they recall inspiration and insight that would otherwise be lost in the current of thought.

Eventually, your research nearly concluded and your desktop full of notes, you will begin to *organise* the material into logical order. How do you do this? As you read through your notes, jot down categories as they emerge, each at the top of a sheet of paper, and write specific information beneath the category headings. You will find that some information wants to go into more than one category. Go ahead at this point and put it in both. You will sort it out later. Some of this preliminary organising will already have begun as you have automatically put some like things together both in your mind and on paper.

Once you have separated out categories, you can order them into a hierarchy of importance, of logical development, or of time. Your purpose in writing will guide the order. This mapping can be difficult because some categories will vie for early position and some will want to fluctuate. Then some information in one early category really should be presented later. These are the organisation problems which will torment you. Just remember, writers are seldom finally pleased with the order in their pieces. Still, one must move on and not edit endlessly. Put things in the order that you think best and move on.

Your categories now in order, you can more deliberately organise the details within them. Here you begin to develop whole paragraphs. You may jump around amid your categories, or you may need to start at the beginning so that you can control the growth of the piece as it will eventually be read. Some people claim that they proceed best by first writing their introductory paragraph, which predicts the whole document. Fine. That paragraph grows naturally out of the thesis statement or the terms of reference (report writing) which you have kept nearby. You may return to that opening paragraph several times and refine it as the essay takes shape and suggests other introductory words. You must find your own mode of operation.

As you have ordered the categories and inserted the appropriate research information, and perhaps a written introductory statement, you are ready to take that first real expository excursion; now write the first rough draft, following the order of your categories, looking frequently at your controlling statement. If this draft seems fairly complete, set it aside and let your mind become clear of the clutter of ideas and alternative phrasings. Come back to it with fresh perspective – only you can decide how long that must be. Read it again to judge what you really have. At this point you proceed critically, cutting and adding where you see the necessity. Like any other craftsperson, you efface and remake portions of your work according to the rules of your craft and in keeping with a coherent plan, until it is right.

Your next draft may be your final one. It depends upon the complexity of your subject and your control over the material. Once you have produced fairly finished text, you must reread for specific technical problems that you have overlooked. Reread for tense uniformity, for agreement between subjects and verbs as well as agreement in number – singular/plural uniformity. You'll be surprised how subtle and slippery agreement is. Reread for appropriate joining of phrases and clauses, for inappropriate idiom and tired clichés, for diction (word choice), for spelling and punctuation. The job is essentially finished at this point. The amount of additional rewriting depends upon the importance of the piece and external constraints of time.

Finished, except for the conclusion. What makes us feel more self-conscious and sometimes insincere than writing a conclusion, which may only reiterate what we've already stated much more eloquently in the body of the text? Conclusions are idiosyncratic. Sometimes they roll out with an inevitability that astonishes a writer. Sometimes they cement an argument. Other times one has nothing more to say, and the conclusion simply restates the opening thesis. The conclusion is a recapitulation of the opening statement that may differ only in the reader's perception. At this point the reader knows more and, therefore, can grasp the statement more fully. Do not underestimate this recap. To produce a good conclusion, you should read the finished essay and, in the rhythm and mood of the piece, move graciously into the closing words. For it is out of the piece of writing that the concluding words will emerge, and so you facilitate that last growth by rereading the whole text – providing it's not a whole book – and letting the conclusion flow out of that final, knowledgeable reading. Once finished, you are given that euphoria which comes with certain moments of completion in all craft. Enjoy it; it's earned.

3. Phrases and Clauses

To begin, we should establish a firm understanding of a few fundamental writing structures. This understanding requires first of all that we make a distinction between phrases and clauses. All writing is made of phrases and clauses.

The Phrase

A phrase is simply a word or a group of words that does not have all the ingredients of a clause. There are many kinds of phrases, and they are all based upon the eight parts of speech. The parts of speech are:

Article
Noun – *common, proper, abstract, and collective*
Pronoun – *stands for a noun*
Verb – *expresses action or a state of being*
Adjective – *tells more about a noun*
Adverb – *tells more about a verb, an adjective, another adverb*
Preposition – *tells position, direction, possession*
Conjunction – *joins phrases and clauses*

Here is a list, based upon the parts of speech, of the different kinds of phrases and examples of each:

Article phrase

a, an, the

Noun phrase

the meeting, a report, a course, documents, the best *project*, David & Sons, Ltd, the recommendation, a careful *conclusion*, the two warring *factions*

Pronoun phrase (*stands for a noun*)

I, you, he, she, it, we, they, me, him, her, us, them, my, mine, your, yours, hers, his, its, our, ours, their, theirs

Verb phrases (*whole verb forms, fully conjugated*)

takes, am/is/are taking, do take, took, have/had taken, will take, will have taken, would have taken, could have taken

Verbal phrases (*a verbal phrase is a partial verb form that lacks a subject*)

taking, taking his good luck for granted, planning their strategy carefully, to get, to get the best results, to keep the competition guessing, given the evidence (The verbal phrase is one of the important writing structures which will be discussed later, see pp. 109–12.)

Prepositional phrase (*always starts with a preposition and ends with a noun*)

in the office, around the table, under a title, of the people, by a writer, beside the coffee cup, next to nothing, for a time, with your consent, to the purpose, over the top, through the correct channels, for a worthy cause

Adjective phrase (*describes a noun*)

pretty red, clearly successful, brilliant, economic, depressed, fairly stable, clear graceful [design], the glossy new well-bound [book]

Adverb phrase

(*describes a verb*): happily, brilliantly, angrily, quickly, well, poorly
(*describes an adjective*): very [happy], absolutely [brilliant], overly [frugal]
(*describes an adverb*): quite [well done], so [well said], too [brashly drawn]

Except for the article, each kind of phrase can have more than one word and still retain its identity – for instance, a noun phrase that has in it an article and an adjective: *the best project*. The adjective, 'best', merely tells more about 'project'; that is its function. But 'project' names something; the whole phrase essentially names a thing and therefore acts as a noun – a noun phrase.

Furthermore, each kind of phrase can function differently in various situations. For instance, a noun phrase can function as a subject, as the object of a verb, as the object of a preposition within a prepositional phrase.

Noun phrase

(*as a subject*): *The engineer's report* recommended a bypass road.
(*as an object of a verb*): The committee considered *the engineer's report*.
(*as an object of a preposition*): The committee adopted the recommendation of *the engineer's report*.

Therefore, each kind of phrase not only derives from a part of speech but also has a grammatical function which is defined by its role or function in the sentence.

Exercise I   *Phrases*

Phrases are linked together. Make up your own.

the brilliant points in the speech
(*adjective, noun, prepositional phrases*)

_____

a chart on top of the page
(*noun, prepositional, prepositional phrases*)

_____

the minutes of the meeting
(*noun, prepositional phrases*)

_____

speaking confidently
(*verbal, adverb phrases*)

_____

asking the students for an essay
(*verbal, noun, prepositional phrases*)

_____

The Clause

A clause is a group of words with both a subject and a properly conjugated verb:

subject + verb

In a clause the subject and verb work together; they agree with one another. This means that the verb is conjugated in the same person as the subject – first person, second person, third person – and is either singular or plural. We are not used to seeing the verbs in our everyday language in a conjugation chart as we study verbs in a new language, yet it may prove useful to look at one. In all of the tenses (times), we lay out the conjugation thus:

TO TAKE (*infinitive form: no person, no time*)
Present tense

	singular	*plural*
First person	I take	We take
Second person	You take	You take
Third person	He ⎫	They take
	She ⎬ takes	
	It ⎭	

For the verb to be properly conjugated it must have its complete form. If the verb is only partially formed, it is called a verbal or participial form.

Complete form	*Verbal form*
I am taking	taking (*participial*)
I have taken	taken (*participial*)
I want to take	to take (*infinitive*)

A clause has the status of being either independent or dependent.

Independent clause

An independent clause has both a subject and a complete verb, and it expresses a finished thought. It stands on its own. It is a sentence.

I want to buy a car.
You must complete your research.

Dependent clause

A dependent clause has also a subject and a complete verb. It does not express a finished thought. It is dependent upon an independent clause to complete its thought. It is not a sentence.

> When *I get* my driving licence . . .
> Because *the essay is due* next week . . .

Now put both the independent and dependent clauses together:

> When I get my driving licence, I want to buy a car.
> Because the essay is due next week, you must complete your research.

Review

All writing is made up of phrases and clauses. A phrase is simply a word or group of words that is not a clause. Each kind of phrase can have different functions in a sentence depending upon its position within the grammatical structure. Thus a noun phrase functions as a subject in the subject position but as an object in the object position.

A clause has both a subject and a properly conjugated verb which agrees with the subject. A clause is either independent, expressing a complete thought and therefore forming a sentence in itself, or dependent, not expressing a complete thought but depending upon an independent clause to finish its thought.

4. The Core of the Independent Clause

Every sentence must have a core – a centre, a base, a heart – to which every addition is attached. A sentence core has a subject plus a properly conjugated verb, and it is contained in an independent clause.

Core = subject + verb *in an independent clause*

When writing a sentence, one keeps the subject always clearly focused in the mind – both the logical and the grammatical subject – and what the subject is doing: the verb. While this sounds painfully simple and clear now, it will soon emerge as a primary consideration that often gets obscured. In Focusing the Subject in chapter 6 on pp. 22–6, we observe how a subject gets lost or locked away from its rightful position, how the sentence focus then gets blurred and, therefore, how the foundation of the whole sentence is weakened.

Core **=** I + take
(*subject*) (*verb*)
Independent clause: *I take* milk in my coffee.

Joining

We add more information ('milk in my coffee') to the core ('I take') by attaching it properly either to the subject or to the verb, or to something further that is properly attached to the core. We build out a sentence by asking a series of questions, starting with the core 'I take':

We ask of the core: I take *what?*
Answer: I take *milk.* (*a direct object of the verb*)

We ask further of the core and its direct object: Where do I take milk?
Answer: I take milk *in my coffee.*

All this attachment in writing is called joining. A writer builds up a sentence by correctly joining phrases and dependent clauses to cores. It all begins with a core, with a subject and its verb. This core is the base of all composition. Whether you are writing or reading, you should always know what the sentence core is; it is the foundation. Therefore, the first real skill in writing comes with the ability to identify and control sentence cores.

A little further development

To the independent clause (IC), 'I take milk in my coffee', we can join a dependent clause (DC), 'because it is too strong just black'. The dependent clause answers the question, why do I take milk in my coffee?

I take milk in my coffee because it is too strong just black. (IC+DC)

Notice that the dependent clause is an unfinished thought in itself, that it finds completion through the independent clause. Notice too that the word *because* both joins the two clauses and makes the second clause dependent upon the first. This is called subordination; *because* is a subordinating conjunction (see chapter 8, Subordinating Statements, pp. 51–7).

Exercise I   *Independent clause cores*

Study these independent clause cores, in which the subject and the verb are set in italics. See also if you can identify complements (See chapter 5, Clause Patterns, pp. 17–21).

1. Limited *liability restricts* the extent to which the members of a business can be held personally liable for the debts of the business.

2. Considering all facets of the report, the *director* finally *made* an informed decision.

3. The *committee*, having deliberated for hours, *considered* him guilty of mismanaging the funds.

4. The *materials had arrived* on time, and the *workers had taken out* their tools.

5. Our *production moved* along efficiently, but the *management gave* us no bonus.

6. The *thrust* of this policy *is outlined* in the White Paper.

7. The *letter is* in the postbox.

8. The *system seems* slow.

9. *These are* his new books.

10. The *librarian* who directed me toward this section of the library *misunderstood* my inquiry. **The Hound of Heaven** is not *shelved* under Pets.

Exercise 2   *Sentence or fragment?*
             Complete or incomplete thought?

Decide which of the following are *complete sentences* **(S)** and which are *fragments* **(F)**. Can you defend your decisions?

1. To curb the losses due to theft, the management installed a surveillance camera system.   _____

2. Follow me.   _____

3. Fearing the consequences of his rash behaviour.   _____

4. Because he needed to finish the paper, having spent every working hour on it for the past week.   _____

5. This is yours.   _____

6. Due to the perseverance of certain politicians.   _____

7. While the report was late, it was happily well researched and written.   _____

8. The chairman calling the meeting back to order.   _____

9. In the heat of the discussion.   _____

10. Wherever there is waste.   _____

11. Why do you delay?   _____

12. Since I have no option.   _____

13. Although I have no option at this time, I will continue to seek a solution.   _____

Solutions are given on p. 159.

5. Clause Patterns

In a broad sense a clause is made of a core plus any phrases properly joined to that core. The clause may be made of only a core (subject + verb alone), or the verb itself may be extended and brought to completion in a complement. A complement completes the action of the verb or expresses a state of being. To include both possibilities, we call both a verb alone and a verb plus its complement the predicate of the clause.

> core   = subject + verb
> clause = subject + predicate (*verb alone or verb + complement*)

The subject and predicate fall into eight basic clause patterns. Observing the following patterns will help you to know how clauses are built in a way that native speakers take for granted. Later we look at how these patterns go wrong and how to repair them (see Predication Problems, p. 30).

Pattern One

SUBJECT	PREDICATE (*intransitive verb: takes no object*)
I	slept.
They	went.
We	dined.
The pen	was hiding.
The lecturer	spoke.
The operator	sat.

Each intransitive verb can take an adverb complement, which tells *how, when, where* the verb is done:

adverb of manner:	I slept *well.*
	They went *quickly.*
	We dined *simply.*
	The lecturer spoke *clearly.*
adverbs of manner and time:	The operator sat *still through the shift.*
adverb of location:	The pen was hiding *behind the cup.*

Pattern Two

SUBJECT	PREDICATE	
	(transitive verb: takes direct object)	
Henry	bound	the report.
The secretary	wrote	the letter.
The postman	carried	the post.
The people	ate	their meal.
The girl	smelt	the rose. *(Notice how 'smell' can be used with or without an object – transitively or intransitively.)*
The tutor	assigned	an essay.
The government	sponsored	an amendment.

Pattern Three

SUBJECT	PREDICATE		
	(transitive verb + indirect object + direct object)		
Martin	sent	me	a memo.
The man	gave	his son	advice.
Eithne	bought	herself	some flowers.
Catherine	told	Sinéad	a secret.
I'll	hand	you	the book.
(implied)	Toss	me	the hole puncher.

Pattern Four

This pattern is the same as Pattern Three except that the verb is one like 'consider' and the *second* noun renames the first noun.

SUBJECT	PREDICATE *(verb + noun + complement)*		
My uncle	considers	me	a fool.
The manager	called	my sister	a genius.
We	supposed	him	an honest man.
The client	thought	ours	a capable firm.

Pattern Five

In the following examples, the verb helps to link the subject to an adjective:

SUBJECT	PREDICATE *(verb + adjective)*	
Ambrose	looked	sad.
The boss	seemed	happy.
The food	tasted	off.
The report	appeared	finished.
The staff	felt	content.
The rose	smelt	sweet.
The patient	grew	troublesome.
The summary	sounded	accurate.

The remaining three cores all use some form of the verb *to be*. Here are the principal parts of this verb:

am, is, are
was, were
shall/will be
is *being*, was being, were being
has *been*, have been, had been, shall/will have been
should/would be, should/would have been

Pattern Six

SUBJECT	VERB *(to be)*	COMPLEMENT *(an adjective)*
The sky	was	clear.
This work	is	tedious.
She	is	competent.
They	are	fast.
The machine	will be	efficient.

Pattern Seven

SUBJECT	VERB (*to be*)	COMPLEMENT (*a noun*)
Tom	was	my colleague.
The third one	is	the building.
This	will be	a good meeting.
She	is	a friendly person.

Pattern Eight

SUBJECT	VERB (*to be*)	COMPLEMENT (*an adverb*)
The treasure	is	here.
The book	was	there.
The children	will be	outside.

		(*prepositional phrases showing location and time*)
The cheque	is	in the postbox.
Their feet	were	under the desk.
Christmas	is	on the 25th of December.
The launch	was	at 6 o'clock.

The Eight Clause Patterns: Review

| Exercise 1 | *The eight clause patterns* |

Write down examples of each of the eight clause patterns.

Pattern One:
Subject + Predicate (*intransitive verb: takes no object*)

Pattern Two:
Subject + Predicate (*transitive verb: takes direct object*)

Pattern Three:
Subject + Predicate (*transitive verb+ indirect object + direct object*)

Pattern Four:
Subject + Predicate (*noun + complement*)

Pattern Five:
Subject + Predicate (*verb+ adjective – 'helping verbs'*)

Pattern Six:
Subject + Verb (*to be*) + complement (*an adjective*)

Pattern Seven:
Subject + Verb (*to be*) + complement (*a noun*)

Pattern Eight:
Subject + Verb (*to be*) + complement (*an adverb*)

6. Focusing the Subject

Focus in the Sentence

Choosing Subjects

A written sentence begins to take shape the moment a subject appears on paper. Therefore, you should make it a point always to choose the best possible subject, so that your sentences are easy for you to write and easy for your reader to follow. Keep the following guidelines in mind.

Prefer active subjects

The subject should be the actor or agent (if there is one). Thus, the *logical subject* should be the *grammatical subject*. Be careful not to bury your real subject in a phrase which you have attached to the core. To find the logical subject, ask yourself what the sentence is primarily about. That should be the subject of your sentence.

Example 1

Poor focus: The *method* of conducting his survey *was to begin interviewing* the least important employees first.

Improved: He *conducted* his survey by interviewing the least important employees first.

While this sentence is partially about a method, a method does not do anything. A method is used or followed by people. In the poor sentence, however, the writer has put 'method' in primary subject position, as though a method could do something, and then was compelled to follow that abstract subject with a weak verb structure, 'was to begin interviewing'. Furthermore, the real verb, 'to conduct', gets buried in a prepositional phrase and so cannot take its rightful position of strength. Once the writer puts a human, active subject into place, an active verb follows and the sentence makes essentially the same statement but now more clearly.

Example 2

Poor focus: The tendency for people not to cheat on their exams comes from fear of getting caught.

Improved: People don't cheat on their exams because they are afraid of getting caught.

Prefer the active voice to the passive voice

How many times has the grammar check on your computer isolated a sentence and stated flatly: 'passive construction' or 'passive voice'? Why does it cite this form and what is it? First, what is the passive voice construction? It has a particular formula:

> *subject* + *a form of to be* + *past participle* + *agent (by whom)*
> The deposit + was + made + by the treasurer.

Writers call this construction the passive voice because the subject does not act; it is acted upon by the agent; the subject remains passive. Because legal and political writers use it, the passive voice has permeated much business and technical writing to the extent that it dominates where the active voice should. In fact, the use of the passive voice has reached such epidemic proportions that computer grammar checks cite it whether it is used appropriately or not. The passive voice does have its benefits.

Uses of the passive voice

(i) The passive voice can help a writer to keep *paragraph focus* in line. Since a writer keeps paragraph focus clear by using consistently linked subjects in all of the sentences, the passive voice construction may prove necessary simply to keep the topic of the paragraph in subject position. For instance, in a paragraph about a lost loan document that a secretary had found, a sentence telling about the discovery would present the document rather than the secretary in subject position:

> The loan document was found by a secretary.

(ii) If the actor or *agent* of the sentence is *unknown* or *unimportant*, then the writer uses the passive voice.

Mr Kelly was given a citation for speeding.
The package was delivered at 11.30 sharp.

(iii) If disclosure of the agent of the action would unduly embarrass
or even damage someone, a writer shows discretion by leaving the
agent out.

Collection of the bill had been overlooked at the end of
the evening. [*The head waiter?*]

Abuses of the passive voice
(i) A writer most obviously abuses the passive voice when he or
she uses it to *obscure* the agent. Consider the insidious implications
of this sentence:

Before your request for a loan can be granted, your
personal finances and credit record will be thoroughly
investigated. [*Oh? By whom? Does the loan officer have a
name?*]

(ii) A writer who uses the passive voice continually – an easy pattern
to get stuck in – has developed a bad stylistic habit. The result is a
vague, stiff, boring style that leaves a reader confused and fatigued
from overwork, the fatigue that comes from continually having to
construe the subject, having to turn sentences around in order to
put the agent into active position, having to fill in gaps the writer
has left, in short, having to do the writer's work. What is the remedy?
The active voice.

Avoid abstract subjects
Generally prefer *human* or *concrete subjects* to abstract or general ones.
Words like method, reason, aspect, explanation, conclusion, situation, attitude usually bring the listless 'is' or 'was' in their wake and
displace the focus of a sentence from what it is really about, some
person or thing.

A human subject is, obviously, one referring to a person. A
concrete subject refers to something one can see, hear, taste, touch,
or smell. Whatever your topic, when you start writing about it,
you likely will find that you are writing about something human or
concrete. There can be no 'education system' without students, lec-
turers, pupils, teachers, classrooms, texts, exams, and exam results;
no 'politics' without voters, ballots, politicians, debates. As you

form a sentence, ask yourself, '*Who* or *what* am I really writing about?' The focus (or grammatical subject) of your sentence should reflect your answer to that question.

Poor focus: The *reason* she filed the document in the wrong folder *was* that it was mistitled.

Improved: *She filed* the document in the wrong folder because it was mistitled.

Consider the verb
In choosing the subject, think of the verb that is to follow it. Usually any active, accurate verb will require a concrete subject, just as the concrete, active subject will demand the right verb.

Rewrite for clarity
If a sentence is causing trouble, look to the subject. Again, ask yourself, 'What exactly am I trying to say?' and make the most direct answer you can. Your answer will provide the best subject for the sentence you are trying to write. The sentence will come out right when you return to the basic core and clarify its subject and its verb.

Avoid putting 'there' in the subject position
The words 'there is' or 'there are' (an expletive) at the beginning of a sentence asserts that something exists. However, since the 'there is/there are' construction comes automatically to mind, as does the passive voice, some writers unconsciously use it in the sentence core and so waste the position where a concrete subject might actively do something. Consider this sentence.

Example 1

> There is a clause in this contract which gives the purchaser the option of withdrawing from the deal within 48 hours.

The real interest lies not so much in the *existence* of the 'clause' (the logical subject), but more in that the clause *gives* an option to the client. As it stands, the subject in this sentence is 'There' and the verb is 'is'. The best subject ('clause') and verb ('gives') for the core of this sentence are locked up respectively in an object position and a dependent clause (adjective clause). We compose a stronger, better focused sentence if we strike the 'there is' and fill the subject and verb positions with active ingredients. (Notice that 'which' disappears also.)

A clause in this contract gives the client the option of withdrawing from the deal within 48 hours.

Example 2

There is a student in this class who wears a red beret and a woollen scarf depicting a piano keyboard.

Again, the interest lies not in the existence of the student but in the wearing of a red beret and keyboard scarf. If we strike out 'There is' and 'who', we will compose a more direct sentence.

A student in this class wears a red beret and a woollen scarf depicting a piano keyboard.

'It' very often works the same way. In the following sentence, for example, the writer has wasted the subject position by filling it with 'it', so that the most appropriate subject is buried in the middle of the sentence.

Example 3

It is in his book, *The Diary of a Writer*, that Dostoevsky describes how a mother hen defended her chickens from a brutal and sadistic boy.

How can we rewrite this sentence so that the real core, 'Dostoevsky describes', gets freed from the dependent clause and takes its proper position in the independent clause? Strike out 'It is' and 'that':

In his book, *The Diary of a Writer*, Dostoevsky describes how a mother hen defended her chickens from a brutal and sadistic boy.

Example 4

It is in his report, *The Circular Relief Road*, that Fitzgerald describes how an inner relief road would lessen inner city congestion and benefit the environment.

Improved:

In his report, *The Circular Relief Road*, Fitzgerald describes how an inner relief road would lessen inner city congestion and benefit the environment.

| Exercise 1 | *Choosing subjects* |

Exercise a little free association by mining each abstraction below for its human or concrete parts.

Examples
Engineering: engineer, drafting table, plan, pencil, ruler, line, scale, construction site, steel, concrete, hard hat, client, contract. . . .
Gardening: soil, roots, bulbs, seeds, trowel, fertiliser, weeds, pests, trellis, flowers. . . .

1. *Politics:*

2. *Discrimination:*

3. *Theatre:*

4. *Finance:*

5. *Chemistry:*

6. *Fashion:*

7. *Law:*

8. *Recreation:*

9. *Honesty:*

10. *The Environment:*

Choosing subjects

Reconstruct these poorly focused sentences, making the logical subject be also the grammatical subject, the name of the person or thing that performs the action of the verb.

1. Something every actor should have is some self-confidence.

2. The result that he hoped to achieve was closing the deal by convincing his client that a delay would mean losing the property.

3. The reason for the confusion of most people with the new regulations is the ambiguous way they are written.

4. The way in which he taught his workers to arrive on time was by locking the doors at 8.01.

5. The method by which the information was acquired by the new researcher was by the use of the Internet.

6. Her expression indicated anger.

7. In *Courage To Be*, by Paul Tillich, it is stated that we only really live when we face the fear of death.

8. It is obvious to those who read them that technical reports should be better written.

9. When a citizen sees that a criminal act is being committed, a telephone call to the police should be placed.

Choosing Verbs

Verbs give writing life because they animate the subject and evoke action in the reader's mind. The more precisely the verb evokes the action of the subject, the more clearly the reader will see exactly what you mean to show. Let's look at several sentences that show an actor entering a stage. Watch how the picture changes as the verbs change.

> The actor *walked out* onto the stage.
> The actor *strolled out* onto the stage.
> The actor *marched out* onto the stage.
> The actor *streaked out* onto the stage.
> The actor *limped out* onto the stage.
> The actor *peeked out* onto the stage.

An accurate verb shows the reader exactly what you want to be seen.

Verbs give a *grammatical action* to your writing. A dynamic verb propels the reader through your sentence whereas a dull, static verb makes your reader trudge through your prose like someone slogging through a bog in a head wind. Compare these two attempts.

> The storyteller gripped the children's attention for two hours and released them still hungry for more.

> During the telling of the story the children were attentive and at the end they were still hungry for more.

The first sentence has more effect because its subject does something a reader can imagine. Furthermore, its verbs – 'gripped' and 'released' – move the sentence along, sparing the reader the plodding lifelessness of the second version.

Exercise 3	*Choosing verbs*

Find a more precise verb to replace the italicised verbs in the following sentences.

1. When confronted with the charge, the culprit lowered his head and, in words we could barely make out, *said* something about having been out of the office that week.

2. Completely enraged, Conor *placed* his hat upon the floor and *spoke* his challenge.

3. Johnson *was done with* the controversial speech, collapsing into the chair and reaching for water.

4. When the children *are* noisy in the library, the librarian must *request* quiet.

5. The sudden appearance of a large shadow from around the corner *disturbed* me.

6. The enthusiastic audience *liked* the compelling speech, which she had *said* with such animation.

7. The disgruntled employees *recited* their complaints outside the factory.

8. Since the new coach took over, *there has been* a deterioration of performance from this team.

A Sentence Off Track: Predication Problems

The predication of a clause is the basic relationship among the words that form the core: the subject, the verb and the complement. When a sentence goes off track, the problem usually starts in the core. Three problems cause the predication in the core of a clause to derail. In this section I will explore these disjunctures and suggest ways to repair them. This section is primarily diagnostic. As a general rule-of-thumb, we change as little as possible when we correct a sentence so that both the sense and the basic structure of the original do not get lost.

Three basic kinds of predication problems

1. *Semantic problem*
The writer has used a standard sentence pattern but has used words in the core position that don't make sense with each other.

Example 1

The true entrepreneur is a firm belief in an enterprise. (*Is an entrepreneur a belief or a believer? Doesn't an entrepreneur have a belief?*)

Solution: The true entrepreneur firmly believes in an enterprise.

Example 2

The report researched three effects of hydrochloric acid on the environment. (*Does a report or a person do research? The sentence needs an accurate subject.*)

Solution: In his report Mr Thompson researched three effects of hydrochloric acid on the environment.

Example 3

The representing agent was an example of duplicity. (*A person can be an example of something but not of a duplicity.*)

Solution: The representing agent practised duplicity.

Example 4

The main factor concerning whether or not a business will survive its start-up period comes under efficient management. (*Does it make sense that a factor comes under anything? Note the abstract subject*)

Solution: Efficient management determines whether or not a business will survive its start-up period.

2. Structure problem
The writer has composed a sentence pattern that doesn't exist in the language.

Example 1

The use of mobile phones in cars is simply as a necessity for many people.

(*In Pattern 8, p. 20, we learnt that a prepositional phrase telling location or time can follow the verb to be. Here, however, 'as a necessity' is a prepositional phrase that expresses neither location nor time, so the core is made of a pattern that does not exist: use . . . is . . . as a necessity. Mobile phones are the necessity, not use.*)

Solution: Mobile phones are simply a necessity for many people.

Or: Many people use mobile telephones as a necessity.

Example 2

The reason he went to the exposition was because he had to
decide upon a new computer system.
(*The core is 'reason . . . was . . . because he had to decide . . . ' :*
subject + to be + dependent clause. This is not a correct pattern. The
problem lies in the phrase, 'the reason', which is taking the place of the
real subject, 'he'. This sentence also shows the earmarks of Problem 3
below. Strike 'the reason' and 'was' in order to fix the sentence.)

Solution: He went to the exposition because he had to decide upon
a new computer system.

Example 3

Opposition to government policies can be in the form of a
peaceful demonstration.
(*Again the wrong structure follows to be. A linking verb such as 'appears',*
or a transitive verb such as 'can take' would correct the problem.)

Solution: Opposition to government policies can take the form of a
peaceful demonstration.

3. Logic problem

The words that logically should make up the core of the sentence do
not, appearing instead as additions to the core, or missing entirely.

Example 1

They were futile in their attempt to gain control over the budget.
(*Are 'they' futile, or is 'their attempt' futile? The writer has buried*
the real subject, 'attempt', inside a prepositional phrase.)

Solution: Their attempt to gain control over the budget was futile.

Example 2

Many Europeans who lived under the Nazi occupation during the
Second World War were a terrible example of human suffering.
(*Are Europeans an example of suffering, or did Europeans suffer terribly?*)

Solution: Many Europeans who lived under the Nazi occupation
during the Second World War suffered terribly.

Example 3

> The level of achievement of some small businesses is on a much
> lower plane than that of others.
> (*Is the level on a lower plane, or is the achievement?*)

Solution: The achievement of some small businesses is on a much
lower plane than that of others.

Example 4

> In relation to the manager and staff, the main conflict was that
> of authority.
> (*Here the real subjects of the sentence, 'the manager and staff', are buried
> in an introductory phrase. They need to be brought out and put into
> subject position.*)

Solution: The manager and staff clashed over authority.
(*Since 'conflict' is really a noun, it should be replaced by a more suitable
verb: 'clashed'.*)

Focus in the Paragraph

Consistent Subjects

A paragraph is a cohesive group of sentences that expands a topic
sentence, which itself is a portion of an introductory thesis statement.
A paragraph first announces a topic and then explains it, describes it,
discusses it, answers it or proves it, often in some combination.
Since all the sentences bear on the paragraph topic, the subjects of
the sentences will often refer to some portion of that topic. If the
paragraph is about an object, most of the sentence subjects in the
paragraph will be nouns naming or pronouns renaming that object.
If the paragraph is about the writer, most of the sentence subjects
will be 'I', and the rest will refer to some aspect of the writer. This
consistency is called focus in the paragraph. Here are several
paragraphs in which I have italicised the focused subject words.

A paragraph about an object:

> Mechanical *machines* work with parts that move. These *parts*
> include levers, gears, belts, wheels, cams, cranks and springs,
> and *they* are often interconnected in complex linkages, *some*
> large enough to move mountains and *others* almost invisible.
> Their *movement* can be so fast that *it* disappears in a blur of

spinning axles and whirling gears, or *it* can be so slow that nothing seems to be moving at all. But whatever their nature, all *machines* that use mechanical parts are built with the same single aim: to ensure that exactly the right amount of force produces just the right amount of movement precisely where it is needed.

DAVID MACAULAY[2]

A paragraph about a person:
I am the other face of Kilbarrack, the other side of Barrytown as represented in **The Commitments**. *I* am in the quiet, hard-working part of working-class culture that very seldom gets a positive representation in the media. *I* also come with loads of new terms. *I* know that I am a carrier of the killer strain; *I* am the voice from below and anathema to those above, hopefully and thankfully. *I* will let in the light or focus a spotlight on a culture that is too often misrepresented and misunderstood. *I* am a community arts worker. *I* want to illustrate how *we* use art as a vehicle for social and community change. In terms of censorship in the arts, *I* will be concentrating on how people in my community, in my social class, experience social control and censorship: education, the arts, language, value judgments, class discrimination, stereotyping and social exclusion.

CATHLEEN O'NEILL[3]

Of course, the sentence subjects of most paragraphs are not as consistent as these. In a paragraph describing Irish woods, the sentence subjects can refer to types of trees, to fauna living in them, to people who look at them, to products made from them and industries growing out of those products.

A paragraph about woods:
Irish woods were famous: varied, dense and impenetrable to the unfamiliar. *Willow, birch, hazel, pine, alder, oak, elm and ash* were predominant, though the concentration varied: *yew* woods in Cork, *oak* in the south-east. *Beech* and *sycamore* followed later; *gorse and hawthorn* really flourished only when the *woods* were cleared, and rampant *exotica* like fuchsia and arbutus were a later development still. In 1600 the *woods* covered about one-eighth of the country; *they* were gradually being cleared, and

by the late sixteenth century *commentators* were already noticing the lack of good mature timber. This was of great economic importance: *pipe staves and barrelling* were vital products. Specialized *work* in wood was widespread (Galway was famous for boat-builders), though *stonemasons* had to be imported; the *woods* were also the basis of the great *glass industry* in Cork and Waterford that was just beginning. Other *industries* rose and fell with the availability of timber; and with the decline of the wood, distinctively Irish *fauna,* like goshawks, deer and wolves, declined too.

R.F. FOSTER[4]

A paragraph about two interrelated things – a service and a customer – will have subjects that alternate between the two. In the following example I have italicised the focus words, even those that are not acting as subjects.

A paragraph about a service and the customer:

A current account is a place where *you* can store money temporarily and make transactions, such as paying bills or cashing cheques. Most *people* have their salary or other income paid directly into their *account*, and then withdraw cash as *they* need it. *You* usually get a chequebook as part of the *package* (unless you are a student), plus a cheque guarantee card which allows *you* to cash cheques of up to £100. *Current account holders* also get a plastic card for withdrawing cash from the 'hole in the wall' (the Automated Teller Machine – ATM). *The associated banks* have far more ATMs than the building societies – almost 800 in total – which gives *you* better access to your money. Furthermore, *banks* normally give overdraft facilities to *clients* who need to borrow money for a short while. *Building societies* do not.

GAIL SEEKAMP[5]

Paragraphs with more complex ideas, paragraphs that argue a point, paragraphs that compare and contrast different things will show less consistency in their sentence subjects than these do. However, a good paragraph will consistently stay within the limits it has imposed by its own topic sentence.

The Topic Sentence: A Review

The topic sentence is usually the first and broadest sentence of each paragraph. It announces to the reader what that paragraph is about. It defines and limits the topic, and it sets up an expectation which the paragraph must satisfy. By generating the paragraph's subject, the topic sentence controls the paragraph's development.

Topic Sentence Checklist

1. It is the broadest, the most general statement in the paragraph (transition statements aside).
2. It states the central idea of the paragraph.
3. It limits and controls the subject matter. In other words, it is narrow or specific enough to be developed in one paragraph.
4. It makes an assertion that requires further explanation, raises questions, or demands proof.
5. It sets up an expectation that can be satisfied. That is, the writer must possess the facts which support the claim that the topic sentence makes.

In the overall scheme of essay organisation, the topic sentence stands midway between the introductory thesis statement and the well-focused sentence subjects within a single paragraph. The topic sentence picks up an aspect of the general thesis of the essay, and each sentence beneath the topic sentence develops that aspect. By this structural scheme the writer is able to focus in for a detailed look at some portion of the general subject and then step back again for a more general view. The scheme allows for controlled, shifting vantages.

Since the topic sentence normally asserts the most general statement in a paragraph, paragraph sentences frequently proceed from the topic sentence in a progression from general to specific. Before studying three kinds of paragraph sequence, you might practise ordering related groups of words in such a progression from general to specific.

Exercise 4   *General to specific*

Rank the words in the following lists. Give 1 to the most general and 5 to the most specific.

A. _____ file _____ office _____ disc _____ programme
_____ building _____ folder _____ computer _____ desk

B. _____ PIN # _____ bank _____ ATM window
_____ current account _____ card

C. _____ writing _____ pen _____ communication
_____ human being _____ language

D. _____ World War I _____ battle _____ historical event
_____ occurrence _____ Battle of Verdun

E. _____ painting _____ work of art _____ The Mona Lisa
_____ Italian painting _____ painting by da Vinci

Exercise 5   *General to specific*

Add to these general sentences another more specific statement that shows more detail about the subject.

A. Our manager gets along with all sorts of people.

B. Caroline is a good researcher.

C. Patrick likes all kinds of music.

D. I felt sick of all the deadline pressure.

E. Travelling is the most attractive feature of my work.

F. The experiment challenged all of my resources.

7. Coordinating Statements

The concept of coordination runs throughout writing. It is fundamental to phrase and clause joining, to paragraph organisation, to essay organisation. In fact, it is one of the three main elements comprising the general principle of organisation.

There are three definitive features of the term *coordinate*:

(i)   to organise diverse elements in a harmonious operation.
(ii) to place [things] in the same class or order.
(iii) to balance two equal weights either side of a centre point.

Coordination in the Sentence

Coordination at the sentence level requires balancing and joining like grammatical structures that have equal weight or importance. This joining is done through the coordinating conjunctions.

The seven coordinating conjunctions

	memory aid	
and	*for*	f
but	*and*	a
yet	*nor*	n
so	*but*	b
or	*or*	o
for	*yet*	y
nor	*so*	s

I strongly recommend that you memorise this list of the seven coordinating conjunctions as a discrete group so that you can always distinguish them from other kinds of conjunctions which may have similar meanings but very different functions. For instance, 'but' and 'although' both express opposition, yet they are different kinds of conjunctions and have very different effects upon the clauses to which they are attached. This distinction will become clearer later.

The two purposes of coordinating conjunctions

(i) Coordinating conjunctions introduce and join coordinate clauses.
All seven coordinating conjunctions can join independent clauses (sentences) and, in so doing, give equal emphasis to each clause and express the logical relationship between the ideas in those sentences. The logical relationship is given in brackets after each example.

1. Sean took CPR, *and* his brother followed his example.
   (addition)

2. Clare took a computer programming course, *but* she couldn't tolerate the hours in front of the monitor. *(opposition)*

3. I wanted to finish the report, *yet* we had one more source to track down. *(opposition)*

4. We needed to get to the theatre on time, *so* I rang for a taxi.
   (cause-effect)

5. You either print out another copy, *or* we will have to share this one. *(alternative)*

6. He printed another copy, *for* they didn't want to share the one.
   (effect–cause)

7. The audience didn't like the speaker, *nor* did the speaker care for the audience. *(negative addition)*

(ii) Coordinating conjunctions join phrases.
Four of the coordinating conjunctions – *and, or, but, yet* – can join elements within the sentence. They

• *join subjects:*	William *or* Edel requested the report.
• *join verbs:*	Edel requested the report *but* rejected its recommendations.
• *join direct objects:*	The staff wanted a new copy machine *and* a better coffee maker.
• *join prepositional phrases:*	He filed the report in the right filing cabinet *yet* in the wrong folder.

Three reasons for learning the seven coordinating conjunctions as a group:

(i) The parts they join together are of equal importance in the sentence; they balance equally weighted thought; they coordinate.

(ii) When a coordinating conjunction joins two independent clauses (complete sentences), we normally put a comma between the two clauses and in front of the coordinator. We do not necessarily do this with other joining words.

(iii) Unlike other joining words, the coordinators can introduce single-clause sentences[6] and thus serve also as transition words (see Transition Words, pp. 61–3). This is true because, when a coordinating conjunction attaches to an independent clause, it does not make that clause an incomplete thought, or a dependent clause. The single clause keeps its independent status; it remains a complete thought; it is still a sentence in itself. In other words, each of the example sentences above could have been written as two complete and separate sentences:

1. Sean took CPR. And his brother followed his example.
2. Clare took a computer programming course. But she couldn't tolerate the hours in front of the monitor.
3. I wanted to finish the report. Yet we had one more source to track down.
4. We needed to get to the theatre on time. So I rang for a taxi.
5. You either print out another copy. Or we will have to share this one.
6. He printed another copy. For they didn't want to share the one.
7. The audience didn't like the speaker. Nor did the speaker care for the audience.

A writer separates and punctuates a coordinate clause in this way to give greater emphasis to the idea in it. If the idea does not deserve such emphasis, the independent clauses should be joined rather than separated, or the conjunction should be removed from the front of the second sentence. As a rule of thumb, one should not begin more than a couple of sentences within any paragraph with a coordinating conjunction. It should be saved for emphasis. And emphasis loses its impact if it gets placed too often. The practice of placing coordinating conjunctions at the beginning of sentences can become a stylistic habit very easily, and they draw attention to themselves in that position. The reader notices and gets distracted. It is like a speaker using the same emphatic hand gesture repeatedly during a speech. Soon people in the audience begin to count the number of times.

Two of the coordinators – *so* and *yet* – can be used a little differently from the others. They can be used together with the co-ordinator *and* to make a two-word coordinator – *and so* and *and yet*:

> I needed a break, *and so* my boss sent me on a holiday to rest.
> There was no reason for a war to take place, *and yet* they went into battle wilfully.

The meaning does not change when one adds the 'and' to 'so' or 'yet'. The tone becomes a little more conversational, but that is the only difference. In formal writing and speaking this conversational tone is usually inappropriate, so one must use discretion.

The Seven Coordinating Conjunctions and the Logical Relationships They Express

Conjunction	*Logical relationship*
and	*Indicates addition* His job brought in several thousand pounds a month [one source of his money], *and* he got another large sum from an inheritance [a second source].
but yet	*Indicates opposition/contrast* She got the job she wanted, *but* she discovered that she hated it. We enjoyed the concert, *yet* many others complained about its length.
so	*Indicates cause-effect* She convinced the committee [cause], *so* she got the position [effect].
or	*Indicates alternative* She will have to find a new job, *or* she will continue to be unhappy. To be *or* not to be. That is the question.
for	*Indicates effect-cause* Charlie had to type the whole essay over [effect], *for* his computer inexplicably erased the original [cause].
nor	*Indicates negative addition* They could find no fault in the system, *nor* did any signs of stress appear on the surface.

| Exercise 1 | *Coordinating conjunctions* |

Using coordinating conjunctions, join the following sentences. Also indicate the logical relationship between the two independent clauses. In these exercises, there are many short examples taken from a variety of situations, so you can repeatedly use the conjunctions in different contexts. The repetition should give you an automatic facility.

logic

1. I play the piano. My sister sings. _____

2. You can work on your proposal.
   We can have a meeting. _____

3. I don't have enough information for my report.
   What I have is not very useful. _____

4. I voted for the man. I still don't like him. _____

5. He took the course twice. He may have to
   take it a third time. _____

6. I hope you'll visit us again soon. We always
   enjoy seeing you. _____

7. I am not going to quit my job. I shall not
   ask for a promotion. _____

8. The company had over-extended its resources.
   The Board recommended cutting expenses. _____

Suggested solutions are given on p. 159.

Exercise 2   *Coordinating conjunctions*

What is wrong with the conjunctions in theses sentences? Can you substitute the correct ones?

1. Sharon always arrives on time, *and* Janet frequently shows up late.

2. We can proceed as we always have, *but* you can propose an alternate plan.

3. The book's binding got dented, *so* it fell off the table.

4. The furniture is very worn, *for* the carpets need replacing.

5. The temperature dropped too quickly, *and* the glass cracked.

6. I found the document that I was looking for, *or* the print was too small to read.

7. I didn't take the book out of the library, *but* I didn't miss it.

Suggested solutions are given on p. 159.

Exercise 3   *Coordinating conjunctions*

Further joining: Using coordinating conjunctions, join the following sentences. Also indicate the logical relationship between the two independent clauses.

                                                                logic

1. There was a thick fog. He had great difficulty finding his way.   _____

2. Joseph shouted out. Nobody heard him.   _____

3. He tried to swim to shore. His clothes dragged him down.   _____

4. Henry had a hard head. Edward had a soft heart. _____

5. The trainer handed him a different racket.
   He began to play much better. _____

6. At the same moment the rain poured down.
   The sun shone through a break in the clouds. _____

7. The fire brigade arrived in ten minutes.
   It was then too late. _____

8. The storm blew down the tree next to the
   house. It crashed through the roof. (*cause-effect*) _____

9. He did not wear an overcoat. He did
   not carry an umbrella. _____

10. I felt quite happy. My proposal had been
    accepted by the committee. _____

11. The director arrived late. The meeting
    was cancelled. _____

12. The road was clear. The crew had
    worked quickly. _____

13. No train ran that day. No bus did either. _____

14. The train stopped. The people got out. _____

15. Jill looked for her lost book. She could
    not find it. _____

16. We hoped to go out for a walk.
    The weather was fine. _____

17. They had to hurry to the station. Their
    friend would miss his train. _____

Suggested solutions are given on p. 159.

Coordinate Sequence Paragraphs

The general principle of organisation holds that the sentence and the paragraph share structural features. A writer not only keeps sentence focus clear by placing the logical subject (what the sentence is about) in the grammatical subject position, but also keeps a paragraph coherent by linking the sentence subjects directly to the topic.

Sentences and paragraphs share another structural parallel in the idea of coordination. Just as clauses of equal importance can be joined together into sentences by the coordinating conjunctions, so too can paragraphs be built out of a series of equally weighted sentences, each kept on the same level of generality, each linked directly to the topic sentence: the coordinate sequence paragraph.

These paragraphs tend to be like lists, and they work well as introductions. Each sentence in a coordinate sequence introductory paragraph can itself open into a whole paragraph and very likely will in the body of an essay or a report. If we rank each sentence in a coordinate sequence paragraph according to its level of generality – the most general being No. 1, and the next more specific being No. 2 – then we can chart graphically how the sentences in this list-like paragraph each develop directly out of the topic sentence. It can be called the 'shopping-list' paragraph. Here is an introductory paragraph that is a deliberate list.

Paragraph 1

> *(a)* The objectives of this book are threefold. *(b)* First, it attempts to describe the overall business environment in Ireland in terms of the business structure, the business environment and the role of the state in industrial development. *(c)* Second, it looks at the four primary industry sectors, namely Traditional, Resource-based, Modern and Services. *(d)* Third, the book attempts to describe the nature of business strategy in the Irish context in terms of strategy formulation and implementation.

> JOHN J. LYNCH AND FRANK W. ROCHE[7]

The list-like scheme of this paragraph is clear as it stands, yet we can look at it more graphically by laying it out with numbers that show the stepping down from a general topic sentence to the examples in the list:

1 *(a)* The objectives of this book are threefold.

2 *(b)*First, it attempts to describe the overall business environment in Ireland in terms of the business structure,
the business environment and the role of the state in
industrial development.

2 *(c)*Second, it looks at the four primary industry sectors,
namely Traditional, Resource-based, Modern and Services.

2 *(d)*Third, the book attempts to describe the nature of business strategy in the Irish context in terms of strategy
formulation and implementation.

General
   1

      2

      2

      2

          Specific

Paragraph 2

The next paragraph works towards its list through a series of
introductory statements which carry the reader from a general
statement to specific views that are given about a certain author. It
does not begin its list until sentence *(d)*. From that point the
remaining sentences are coordinate.

(a) An age in which one set of emotional and moral standards
is normal may find strange what another time considered
acceptable and even commendable. *(b)* This is especially true
as regards Henry Mackenzie's *The Man of Feeling*. *(c)* Since its
publication in 1771, literary critics have differed widely in their
opinions of the book's merits. *(d)* Edmund Gosse announced
that Mackenzie had neither knowledge of the world nor
observation of life; *(e)* Henry Morley amused himself and his
readers by indexing the occasions on which Mackenzie's characters shed tears. *(f)* Yet J.M.S. Tompkins (*The Popular Novel in
England,* p.54), whose scholarship is probably superior to that
of both earlier men, called it 'the most perfect and most
conscious expression after Sterne, of that type of novel which
relies for interest on a delicate variety of emotional hue.'

KENNETH C. SLAGLE[8]

This paragraph begins as a subordinate sequence – the next type to be discussed – but it is dominated by a coordinate sequence structure.

Paragraph 3

The next paragraph is an introductory paragraph, the first in the book from which it is taken. It acts like an overture to the whole book and, therefore, contains kernels of the book's topics, each of which will be unfolded in the chapters and paragraphs which follow. Notice how the writer gathers and controls a wealth of material by using consistent subjects.

(a) Kate O'Brien is a pioneer. *(b)* She is the first writer of Irish fiction to represent fully and meticulously the Catholic upper-middle class. *(c)* And her innovation goes further. *(d)* She is the first to address issues common among Irish women of the twentieth century and to introduce into Irish literature questions of female autonomy, self-definition, and sexual freedom that current writers, such as Edna O'Brien, Julia O'Faolain, and Val Mulkerns continue to address. *(e)* Further still, she tenders the earliest female version of the Irish artistic quest that serves as a compelling analogue to the masculine experience explored initially by James Joyce, in *A Portrait of the Artist as a Young Man,* and later by such writers as Sean O'Faolain, in *Bird Alone,* and John McGahern, in *The Dark.* *(f)* And finally, as deeply committed to Ireland as any of her male literary colleagues, residents and expatriates alike, Kate O'Brien scrutinises, even from long distance, the dominant social and political problems that beset her homeland. *(g)* As do many of her male contemporaries, she consistently portrays the land and *mentalité* she sought to escape. *(h)* But Kate O'Brien's Ireland differs profoundly from theirs, and her singular perspective warrants a prominent place in Irish letters.

ADELE M. DALSIMER[9]

Paragraph 4

A writer can use this coordinated paragraph arrangement, the list, in the middle of a document when summing up a series of points before going on to new territory. Or a writer may simply need to chronicle a mass of impressions as in this midway paragraph from 'Here is New York', by E.B. White. Notice that the first two sentences both inhabit the same level of generality before White launches into his list of features. I have italicised focus words that refer to people and the place.

(a) It is a miracle that *New York* works at all. *(b)* The whole *thing* is implausible. (c) Every time the *residents* brush their teeth, millions of gallons of water must be drawn from the Catskills and the hills of Westchester. (d) When a young *man* in Manhattan writes a letter to his girl in Brooklyn, the *love message* gets blown to her through a pneumatic tube – pfft – just like that. *(e)* The *subterranean system* of telephone cables, power lines, steam pipes, gas mains, and sewer pipes is reason enough to abandon the island to the gods and the weevils. *(f)* Every time an incision is made in the pavement, the *noisy surgeons* expose ganglia that are tangled beyond belief. [This is the only sentence that breaks the coordinate sequence. It steps down to a more specific level.] *(g)* By rights *New York* should have destroyed itself long ago, from panic or fire or rioting or failure of some deep labyrinthine short circuit. *(h)* Long ago *the city* should have experienced an insoluble traffic snarl at some impossible bottleneck. *(i)* *It* should have perished of hunger when food lines failed for a few days. *(j)* *It* should have been wiped out by a plague starting in its slums or carried in by ships' rats. *(k)* *It* should have been overwhelmed by the sea that licks at it on every side. *(l)* The *workers* in its myriad cells should have succumbed to nerves, from the fearful pall of *smoke-fog* that drifts over every few days from Jersey, blotting out all light at noon and leaving the high offices suspended, *men* groping and depressed, and the sense of world's end. *(m)* *It* should have been touched in the head by the August heat and gone off its rocker.

E.B. WHITE[10]

Paragraph 5

The coordinate sequence also can be used for conclusions when a writer reiterates points that have been explored in the body of the text.

(a) Be that as it may, this kind of detail about what men thought and said at the time dots almost every page of Gilbert's book, shows how different the world was 60 or 70 years ago, and brings his account to life. *(b)* In short, we have here a fascinating

treatment that we can all profit by dipping into, and which A-level and undergraduate students will find particularly valuable. *(c)* I congratulate Gilbert on his good work, and look forward to the next two volumes.

PAUL JOHNSON[11]

While it is quite simple, the coordinate sequence is a useful paragraph structure. It allows a writer to predict in a list what will follow, to present a series of equally important statements, to reiterate what has been explored, to sum up. It does not, however, allow a writer to delve into the details of a subject. That movement belongs to the subordinate sequence paragraph.

8. Subordinating Statements

Like coordination, the idea of subordination runs all through writing. Both kinds of relations — equal status and unequal status — continually present themselves in the written line. While composing, a writer is continually deciding what is important and what is background, or secondary, or subordinate. Subordinate structure puts one idea into the background in order to bring another idea forward. Subordination is the second of the three main elements in the general principle of organisation.

As for the term coordinate, there are three distinctive features of the term *subordinate*:

(i)   of a lesser importance
(ii)   under the authority or control of another
(iii)   dependent upon another

Subordination in the Sentence

Subordination in the sentence expresses the relation between independent and dependent clauses. A subordinate, or dependent, clause — the terms are interchangeable — is not only less important than the independent clause to which it is joined but also dependent upon the independent clause to finish out its thought. Taking a subordinate position, it allows the independent clause to receive more emphasis than itself.

It is the subordinating conjunction that makes a clause subordinate. Observe the difference:

Example 1

> I found the book I was looking for.
> *Although* I found the book I was looking for.

Although is a subordinating conjunction which makes the thought of its clause unfinished and dependent upon another clause to finish it:

> *Although* I found the book I was looking for, I didn't find the quotation I wanted.

The chief effects of the subordinating conjunction

(a) to make the thought of a clause incomplete;
(b) to make a clause dependent upon an independent clause to finish its thought;
(c) to make the dependent clause less important than the independent clause (to subordinate it), and to give emphasis to the independent clause.

The subordinating conjunction allows you to show your reader where you're placing the *emphasis*. This conjunction gives you, the writer, greater control and flexibility. Compare these three versions.

Example 2

equally balanced: Niamh misses work at least once a week, *yet* she does an excellent job on all her assignments. (*shows balanced opposition*)

emphasis placed: *Although* Niamh misses work at least once a week, she does an excellent job on all her assignments. (*Her excellent performance is emphasised*)

alternative: *Niamh misses work at least once a week although* she does an excellent job on all her assignments. (*Missing work is emphasised*)

There are many subordinating conjunctions. There is less need to memorise them in a list than there is to remember the coordinating conjunctions as a group. The best approach is to learn how these joining words function in a sentence. Some of the most common ones are:

because   although   if   while
as   since   when   whereas   unless

How subordinating conjunctions function

(a) Subordinators attach themselves to the front of clauses
While coordinators always go between independent clauses to join them, subordinators do not. Instead, a subordinator attaches itself to the front of a clause. That dependent clause can be placed first in the sentence, so the subordinator appears at the beginning of the whole sentence, telling the reader that the first clause is dependent and that two clauses are being joined together into one sentence.

> *Because* I found the book I was looking for, I was able to find the quotation I wanted.

Of course, the order of the clauses can be reversed. (*Notice that the comma disappears.*)

> I was able to find the quotation I wanted *because* I found the book I was looking for.

(b) Subordinators cannot introduce a single-clause sentence
Unlike a coordinating conjunction, which can introduce a single-clause sentence, a subordinating conjunction cannot. Rather, it makes a clause unable to stand independently as a complete sentence because the subordinator makes the thought incomplete. Compare:

Example 3

COORDINATORS
She entered the shop.	(*sentence*)
And she entered the shop.	(*sentence*)
For she entered the shop.	(*sentence*)
Or she entered the shop.	(*sentence*)
But she entered the shop.	(*sentence*)

SUBORDINATORS
She entered the shop.	(*sentence*)
Because she entered the shop,	(*not a sentence*)
If she entered the shop,	(*not a sentence*)
Although she entered the shop,	(*not a sentence*)
While she entered the shop,	(*not a sentence*)

The cast of a whole paragraph will be determined by the placement of a subordinating conjunction. Consider these two sentences:

Example 4

> The solution to the firm's problem is very simple.
> The causes are complex.

What direction would a paragraph take given this way of stating the observation?

> *Even though* the solution to the firm's problem is very simple, the causes are complex.   (*stresses complex causes*)

And this other way?

> The solution to the firm's problem is very simple *even though* the causes are complex.   (*stresses simple solution*)

Example 5   A LITERARY EXAMPLE

two sentences: John Donne used plain language in his poetry. His metaphors are extremely complex, however. ('However' is a transition word, not a conjunction – See Transition Words, pp. 61–3.)

one way: Even though John Donne used plain language in his poetry, his metaphors are extremely complex.
(*stresses complex metaphors*)

another way: John Donne used plain language in his poetry even though his metaphors are extremely complex.
(*stresses plain language*)

How would a paragraph develop given the first way of stating the observation? the second?

(c) The importance of placement
What is wrong with the following sentence?

Example 6

> John arrived early at the office where an important FAX was waiting *because he had lots of work to finish.* (*The questionable subordinate clause is italicised.*)

The sentence is made of three clauses:

> John arrived early at the office (*independent*)
> where an important FAX was waiting (*dependent*)
> *because he had lots of work to finish.* (*dependent*)

A STRUCTURAL RULE: A subordinate clause affects (modifies) the clause nearest to it. As it stands, the example sentence about John actually states that his having lots of work causes an important FAX to wait. But the writer meant to say that his having lots of work causes John to arrive early at the office. For the sake of clarity and accuracy, the italicised dependent clause should be moved to the front of independent clause: 'John arrived early at the office'. The improved sentence:

> *Because he had lots of work to finish,* John arrived early at the office where an important FAX was waiting.

'Where an important FAX was waiting' is also a dependent clause – see chapter 11, Adjective Clauses, pp. 98–104 – that tells more about 'office'. It needs to go next to 'office' so that it comes close to the word it modifies. The italicised clause cannot go between 'office' and the adjective clause, so it must go to the front of the independent clause.

(d) A little punctuation
(i) When a subordinate clause begins a sentence, it is followed by a comma.

Example 7

> *Because* he was late, he missed the train.
> *Although* she listened to his excuses, she felt no sympathy.

(ii) A subordinate clause is not set off from the independent clause by a comma when it comes at the end of the sentence unless the independent clause is unusually long.

> He missed the train *because* he was late.
> She felt no sympathy *although* she listened to his excuses.

(iii) A subordinate clause, when it comes in the middle of an independent clause, is almost always surrounded by commas (as in this sentence and in Example 8).

Example 8

> She felt, *although* she listened to his excuses, no sympathy.
> We thought, *even though* we had plenty of evidence to
> the contrary, that he was guilty.

(e) Logical connections

Subordinators show some logical relationships that coordinators also
show, but they show others that coordinators cannot.

(i) Like the coordinators *but* and *yet,* some subordinators can show
opposition:

Example 9

> We were happy, *but* we lost the account.
> We were happy *although* we lost the account.
> *While* we lost the account, we were happy.

(ii) Others can show effect–cause or cause–effect as do *for* and *so*:

Example 10

> She consulted John, *for* he had the expertise. (*effect-cause*)
> She consulted John *because* he had the expertise. (*effect-cause*)
> He had the expertise, *so* she consulted John. (*cause-effect*)
> *Since* he had the expertise, she consulted John. (*cause-effect*)

(iii) Subordinators cannot show addition as *and*, or alternatives as *or*.
Yet they can show time and condition, relations which no coordinator can show:

Example 11

Time	*Condition*
When you get there, I'll be gone.	*Unless* we hurry, we are going to be late.
After you've gone, I'll be sorry.	You can succeed at learning French *if* you really want to.
Don't leave the office *until* the memo is sent.	
You may go *as soon as* you are finished.	

Common subordinating conjunctions and the logical relationships they express

Conjunction	*Logical Relationship*
because since as now that	cause and effect
though, although, even though while whereas even if no matter how	contrast
if unless provided that in case	condition
as, as if, as though	comparison
so that in order that	purpose
after since when, whenever while before until as as long as, as soon as now that	time
whatever wherever	miscellaneous

| Exercise 1 | Subordinate clauses |

Underline the subordinate clauses in the following sentences:

1. I silently uttered a short prayer as the invigilator passed out the exam booklets.

2. I tried reading my science textbook as if it were pleasure reading.

3. As the chartered airliner made its landing approach, I counted my blessings.

4. When my infatuation passed, I realised what a fool I had been.

5. After the dentist had propped my mouth open, squirted all kinds of vile-tasting solutions into it, and filled it with various metal implements, he decided to begin a friendly chat.

6. Although Dr Mallory delivers his lectures at a rate of 173 words a minute in an effort, he says, to save time, he only ends up repeating himself at least three times because no one can make out what he is saying.

| Exercise 2 | The Logic of subordination |

1. Which of the following would be written by *an optimist?*

   (a) Although the crime rate is very high, humans have progressed in many ways.
   (b) Although humans have progressed in many ways, the crime rate is very high.

2. Writing on the *causes of the fall of the Roman Empire,* which would a historian be more likely to write?

   (a) After the Roman Empire was considerably weakened, corruption in high places became widespread.
   (b) After corruption in high places became widespread, the Roman Empire was considerably weakened.

3. Which expresses *more determination*?

(a) Although a lifetime is short, much can be accomplished.
(b) Although much can be accomplished, a lifetime is short.

4. In which sentence did he apparently *overcome his speech defect*?

(a) In spite of the fact that he had a speech defect, Cotton Mather became a great preacher.
(b) In spite of the fact that he became a great preacher, Cotton Mather had a speech defect.

5. Which sentence indicates *accidental discovery*?
(a) While he took a bath, Archimedes formulated one of the most important principles of physics.
(b) While he formulated one of the most important principles of physics, Archimedes took a bath.

Exercise 3   *Subordinating conjunctions*

Join each of the two sentences together into one sentence by using one of the subordinating conjunctions. Consider which clause contains the more important information. Often there will be several possible joining solutions. Decide upon one that works logically. Refer to the summary of subordinating conjunctions for options and for the logic expressed by the conjunction. (I have suggested a logic for some.)

1. It was over. We had lost half of our accounts and a dozen employees. (*time/effect-cause*)

2. You take the bus just outside. You will be taken to City Centre. (*condition*)

3. You will have to wait. I am finished.

4. You will have to work late. You didn't finish the project.

5. We read through the draft. We found gross errors in the calculations.

6. I have finished my essay. We can go to lunch.

7. We had interviewed people all day. We found no one suitable for the position.

8. I have photocopied your memo. We can distribute it among all the staff. (*purpose*)

9. The supervisor thinks the workers waste too much time in breaks. Everyone else thinks he's Scrooge.

10. I spent most of my weekends in Hong Kong or Bangkok. They were only an hour and a half away.

11. You look into this problem. You notice all sorts of inconsistencies in accounting.

Exercise 4   *Subordination*

Change the joining in the following sentences by using some form of subordination instead of coordination.

1. My supervisor did not approve of my proposal, *so* I drafted a more modest one.

2. Our advertising strategy was brilliant, *yet* the general economic picture proved bleak.

3. The auctioneer always got high bids, *for* he knew the qualities of fine furniture intimately.

4. Martin tried hard to impress his new boss, *but* she thought he was hopeless.

5. The book contained no pictures or illustrations, *so* it bored me.

6. Robert Schumann wrote lieder, quartets, piano music and symphonies, *yet* his best known work is a piano concerto.

7. Little Susie preferred the day after Christmas *and* she could play with her toys.

| Exercise 5 | *Situations* |

1. You're annoyed at the discourteous treatment you received the last time you were in the stereo shop and decide to write the manager a letter about it. Using a subordinate clause, write a sentence in which you acknowledge the good service you have generally received there, but *emphasise your displeasure* over the recent incident.

| SC | , | IC |
| good service acknowledged , | | displeasure emphasised |

2. Your supervisor has asked you for a progress report on your research, which you have only just begun, and has asked for it to be on his desk impossibly soon. Using a subordinate clause, write a sentence in which you express your willingness to give him a report but emphasise that there hasn't been enough time to accomplish anything to report.

| SC | , | IC |
| willing to give report | , | too little time emphasised |

Transition Words

People often ask if 'however' or 'therefore' are subordinating conjunctions. They are not even conjunctions because they do not join structures. In fact they have no grammatical role in the sentence. Their purpose is entirely rhetorical; they are transition words. They can be taken out of a sentence and put back in without ever affecting the sentence's grammatical structure. Nothing falls if they leave; nothing depends upon their presence. Still, they are very useful and give a grace to the writing if they are used well, that is appropriately and sparingly.

Because they are not part of the grammatical structure of a sentence, transition words are 'free'. And as you will see in adjective clause usage, a 'free modifier' is always set off by commas or other appropriate punctuation. This marking shows that the transition word is not an integral part of the structure but an insertion that could be removed without any loss to the essential sense of the sentence. Thus, an important feature of the transition words is that they need to be marked, front and back, by some kind of punctuation.

Demonstration using 'however'

There are three kinds of punctuation that set off a transition word:

. However, (a full stop and a comma)
; however, (a semicolon and a comma) (See Punctuation
          for semicolon, p. 131)
, however, (a comma and a comma)

The first two ways occur when the transition word comes between independent clauses and a full stop or semicolon would normally be needed. Remember, since a transition word is not a conjunction, it cannot join clauses.

> The committee adopted the measure. *However,* there was some dissent from a few members.
>
> *or:* The committee adopted the measure; *however,* there was some dissent from a few members.

Within a single clause, let's say between the subject and verb, the transition word needs to be set off only by commas:

> There was some dissent from a few members. The committee, *however,* adopted the measure.

Transition words and their sense

Transitions marking time	*Transitions showing addition*
meanwhile	furthermore
at first	in addition
finally	moreover
subsequently	further
initially	also
to begin with	another
then	at the same time
next	beyond
suddenly	
at that moment	

Transitions expressing contrast	*Transitions indicating result*
however	as a result
nevertheless	consequently
on the other hand	therefore
still	accordingly
thus	

Transitions giving emphasis

more important
most important
significantly
surprisingly

Subordinate Sequence Paragraphs

As in the sentence, so in the paragraph. As we saw in clause subordination, a writer frequently makes one statement subordinate to and dependent upon another. So in a subordinate sequence paragraph, a similar dependency develops as the paragraph moves from a general topic sentence to a more specific statement which grows out of the topic sentence, and then to another more specific sentence which grows out of that previous one, and so on. Instead of looking like a shopping list of equally important but related items (coordinate sequence), the subordinate sequence paragraph looks more like a staircase on which the reader and writer descend from the topmost general topic sentence to the bottom-most specific statement. The last sentence could not follow directly from the topic sentence but, by a series of connected statements, is linked to it by steps.

Paragraph 1
The following paragraph by Bernice Grohskopf shows the stepping down from general to specific very clearly.

(a) The fundamentals of archaeology cannot be condensed in a chapter, or even in one book. (b) Webster defines archaeology as 'the scientific study of the life and culture of ancient peoples, as by excavation of ancient cities, relics, artifacts, etc.' (c) But an artifact has no historical value until it can be identified and placed in time. (d) Thus, the archaeologist's concern is not merely with finding relics, but with finding out about them. (e) He must not only know techniques of excavation, but he must have a thorough knowledge of the history and the language of the people and the period he is studying. *(f)* A specialist in classical archaeology, for instance, might know how to conduct an excavation in Mexico, or England – exactly how to approach a site so as to prevent damage to objects, how to take notes with diagrams and maps – but he would probably know very little about what he found.

BERNICE GROHSKOPF[12]

Notice that in each sentence she repeats or refers to a word or a phrase from the previous sentence and develops it. Below I have italicised the words which show the links from sentence to sentence as the paragraph develops. I have also set the paragraph in a step format to show the descending levels of generality.

[General]

1 *(a)* The fundamentals of *archaeology* cannot be condensed in a chapter, or even in one book.

2 *(b)* Webster defines *archaeology* as 'the scientific study of the life and culture of ancient peoples, as by excavation of ancient cities, relics, *artifacts*, etc.'

3 *(c)* But an *artifact* has no historical value until it can be *identified and placed* in time.

4 *(d)* Thus, the archaeologist's concern is not merely with finding relics, but with *finding out about them.*

5 *(e)* He must not only know techniques of excavation, but he must have a *thorough knowledge of* the history and the language of the people and the period he is studying.

6 *(f)* A *specialist* in classical archaeology, *for instance,* might know how to conduct an excavation in Mexico, or England – exactly how to approach a site so as to prevent damage to objects, how to take notes with diagrams and maps – but he would probably know very little about what he found.

[Specific]

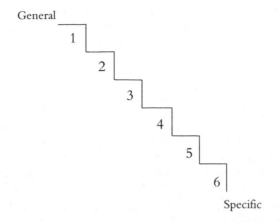

General

1

2

3

4

5

6

Specific

Paragraph 2
Here is a short paragraph which develops as one thought suggests another. It seems to follow a logic of consequences.

> *(a)* A mortgage is the biggest financial commitment you make in your life. *(b)* Mortgage arrears are a common form of debt among middle-income earners. *(c)* The current economic boom has seen a dramatic increase in the amount of debt, particularly for mortgages and large loans. *(d)* This situation led the Central Bank to caution lenders about the dangers of excessive mortgage lending.

MARK TIERNEY[13]

1 *(a)* A *mortgage* is the biggest financial commitment you make in your life.
  2 *(b)* *Mortgage arrears* are a common form of *debt* among middle-income earners.
    3 *(c)* The current economic boom has seen a *dramatic increase* in the amount of *debt*, particularly for mortgages and large loans.
      4 *(d)* *This situation* led the Central Bank to caution lenders about the dangers of excessive mortgage lending.

Paragraph 3
The next paragraph, from Erich Auerbach's *Mimesis,* follows a narrative line. I do not italicise focus words, so you can trace the links and observe the stepping down through the narrative yourself.

(a) Readers of the *Odyssey* will remember the well-prepared and touching scene in book 19, when Odysseus has at last come home, the scene in which the old housekeeper Euryclea, who had been his nurse, recognizes him by a scar on his thigh. *(b)* The stranger has won Penelope's good will; at his request she tells the housekeeper to wash his feet, which, in all old stories, is the first duty of hospitality toward a tired traveler. *(c)* Euryclea busies herself fetching water and mixing cold with hot, meanwhile speaking sadly of her absent master, who is probably of the same age as the guest, and who perhaps, like the guest, is even now wandering somewhere, a stranger; and she remarks how astonishingly like him the guest looks. *(d)* Meanwhile Odysseus, remembering his scar, moves back out of the light; *(e)* he knows that, despite his efforts to hide his identity, Euryclea will now recognize him, but he wants at least to keep Penelope in ignorance. *(f)* No sooner has the old woman touched the scar than, in her joyous surprise, she lets Odysseus' foot drop into the basin; the water spills over, she is about to cry out her joy; *(g)* Odysseus restrains her with whispered threats and endearments; *(h)* she recovers herself and conceals her emotion. *(i)* Penelope, whose attention Athena's foresight had diverted from the incident, has observed nothing.

ERICH AUERBACH[14]

Paragraph 4
Taken from a business management text, the following paragraph is packed with information, yet we can clearly see its sequence of steps into further detail.

(a) The basis for the *Single Market* is the unhampered movement between member states of persons, goods, services and capital. *(b)* In order for *this market* to function effectively, great *changes in member states' regulatory systems* had to occur, and many of these structural changes are now in place or are well advanced. *(c)* In 1987, a major *step towards European integration* took place when Ireland's ratification of the *Single European Act* (SEA) enabled all the complex set of mechanisms which had evolved to create a true Common Market. *(d)* The *SEA went further*, providing a public statement of intent to continue the process of integration, and it provided for many *new mechanisms* to allow this to take place. *(e)* In 1992 the *Maastricht*

Agreement paved the way for clearer political and economic union among the member states.

JOHN J. LYNCH AND FRANK W. ROCHE[15]

Paragraph 5
In a different mode, a paragraph from *The Sunday Times* recounts the development of an industry: the ski resort.

(a) On the whole the French have never been complacent about their *lift systems* or ski areas. *(b)* They have always looked to replace an *old slow lift* with a *new fast one* at the earliest opportunity and have constantly looked at ways of expanding their already vast ski areas still further. *(c)* This is only sensible, since as *lifts speed up*, so the amount of *ground skiers can cover in a day* gets greater and with it their eagerness for new challenges. *(d) Twenty years ago it took* an early start, a short lunch and the *whole skiing day* for a decent intermediate skier to get from Courchevel 1850, at one end of the Trois Vallées lift system, to Val Thorens at the other end and back again. *(e) Today,* thanks to the new lifts, the same skier could do the return journey easily *in half a day. (f)* Partly *for this reason,* the *Trois Vallées has* recently *begun to expand* into a fourth valley, the Maurienne, in order to provide yet more variety.

ALISTAIR SCOTT [16]

Paragraph 6
Another subordinate sequence paragraph shows a geologic development:

(a) The key to understanding much of Ireland's physical habitat and personality lies in its *geographical location. (b)* Now a relatively small *island located* on the north-west edge of the European mainland, between 51.5 and 55.5 degrees north latitude and 5.5 and 10.5 degrees west longitude, Ireland was once *part of that larger land mass. (c)* As a result, its geological structure and surface land forms *share many features* in common with the neighbouring island of *Great Britain* and with north-western *France. (d)* Ireland remained connected to *Britain* by a *land bridge* at the end of the last major Ice Age when Britain remained similarly joined to *continental Europe. (e) The land link* with Britain *disappeared* beneath the rising level of the Irish

Sea some time after 10,000 years ago. *(f)* The *breaking of the land link with Britain* brought to an end the overland migration of *flora and fauna* to Ireland. *(g)* Many *species of plants and some animals* which subsequently reached Britain from mainland Europe failed to arrive in the more westerly island.

MARY CAWLEY[17]

Subordinate sequence paragraphs show the development of thought as it takes a general point and works it into detail. Following the bare links between sentences, we can quickly see a summary of the paragraph's contents. Furthermore, by studying the paragraphs of other writers in this way, we can discover models for our own paragraph mapping.

Writing a subordinate sequence paragraph is an exercise in making logical connections from sentence to sentence and a process of refining a topic down to its smaller parts. A writer wants to say something specific and precise, and the way to guide a reader to that specific point starts with a general orientation, takes a series of descending steps, each one picking up a piece of the previous step, and finally lands securely on the point toward which the whole paragraph has logically moved. This takes deliberate practice and requires a critical eye in the writer, who constantly asks, 'Is what I have on the paper, on the screen, all that I need to say? Have I left a step out? Or have I put in any distractions that will misguide the reader? Where am I out of step?' A great test of continuity and coherence for the writer is the subordinate sequence paragraph.

Of course, no scheme can ever cover all the possibilities of rich, coherent expression in writing. Thought is complex, often far reaching, and writing must retain its flexibility in order to manipulate the depth and volume of any subject matter. Nevertheless, formal schemes do help a writer roughly to organise statements of thought and information, so we turn now to the next kind of sequence in paragraph construction: the mixed sequence.

9. The Mixed Sequence Paragraph

A mixed sequence paragraph combines coordinate and subordinate statements. This mixture of the two is the third element in the general principle of organisation.

Once the topic sentence sets the parameters of the paragraph, the sentences beneath it can develop in a number of ways. The second sentence normally takes the paragraph to the next specific level, No. 2. It can be followed by another sentence either on the same level (No. 2: *coordinate*) or onto the next level down the stairs of specificity (No. 3: *subordinate*). While the paragraph goes down the steps towards more specific detail, it can linger on one level in coordinated statements or jump back at any time to a more general level and be coordinate with an earlier sentence in the paragraph. Here is a visual representation of only a few mixed sequence possibilities.

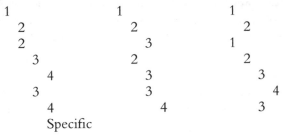

Paragraph 1
Below is a coordinate sequence paragraph about artists. It opens with a general statement about them and then presents three examples. At this point the paragraph does not give any detail about each artist.

(a) All artists quiver under the lash of adverse criticism.
(b) Rachmaninoff's first symphony was a failure, so he took sick.
(c) When Beethoven heard that a certain conductor refused to perform one of his symphonies, he went to bed and stayed there until the symphony was performed. (d) Charles Dickens was forever defending himself against criticism, writing letters to the press and protesting that he was misunderstood.[18]

This has a simple coordinate sequence pattern:

(a) 1
(b)   2
(c)   2
(d)   2

However, in the example above I have removed from the original paragraph the sentences that develop the level No. 2 sentences. We can see how the writer internally developed the paragraph if we restore those sentences which show more about two of the artists. The restored sentences appear in italics.

(a) All artists quiver under the lash of adverse criticism. *(b)* Rachmaninoff's first symphony was a failure, so he took sick. *(c) He lay around on sofas for a year, without writing one measure of music. (d) But he eventually recovered, and went on to write much more music. (e)* When Beethoven heard that a certain conductor refused to perform one of his symphonies, he went to bed and stayed there until the symphony was performed. *(f)* Charles Dickens was forever defending himself against criticism, writing letters to the press and protesting that he was misunderstood. *(g) Yet neither criticism nor misunderstanding stopped his output.*

1 *(a)* All artists quiver under the lash of adverse criticism.
  2 *(b)* Rachmaninoff's first symphony was a failure, so he took sick.
    3 *(c)* He lay around on sofas for a year, without writing one measure of music.
      4 *(d)* But he eventually recovered, and went on to write much more music.
  2 *(e)* When Beethoven heard that a certain conductor refused to perform one of his symphonies, he went to bed and stayed there until the symphony was performed.

2 *(f)* Charles Dickens was forever defending himself against criticism, writing letters to the press and protesting that he was misunderstood.

　3 *(g)* Yet neither criticism nor misunderstanding stopped his output.

(a)	1		
(b)	2		
(c)		3	
(d)			4
(e)	2		
(f)	2		
(g)		3	

(a) 1
(b) 　2
(c) 　　3
(d) 　　　4　　　(*lower levels = more detail*)
(e) 　2
(f) 　2
(g) 　　3

The following two paragraphs, appearing in succession to each other within an essay, are both mixed sequences. The first is based upon a subordinate sequence model and the second is based on the coordinate sequence.

Paragraph 2

Based upon a subordinate sequence model:

(a) Investing in property is beyond the reach of many people with a mortgage to pay and children to support. *(b)* Most of us – even if we have no dependents – can only afford to pay one mortgage, and it's unwise to treat your own home as a speculative investment. *(c)* The property market is subject to booms and crashes. *(d)* You may make a profit each time you sell your house to get a bigger one. *(e)* But some people who 'trade up' find themselves saddled with a huge mortgage if property values fall after they move. *(f)* If the market value of your house falls below the size of your mortgage, you are said to have 'negative equity' in your home.

GAIL SEEKAMP[19]

1 *(a)* Investing in property is beyond the reach of many people with a mortgage to pay and children to support.
　2 *(b)* Most of us – even if we have no dependents – can only afford to pay one mortgage, and it's unwise to treat your own home as a speculative investment.
　　3 *(c)* The property market is subject to booms and crashes.

4 *(d)* You may make a profit each time you sell your house to get a bigger one.

4 *(e)* *But* some people who 'trade up' find themselves saddled with a huge mortgage if property values fall after they move.

5 *(f)* If the market value of your house falls below the size of your mortgage, you are said to have 'negative equity' in your home.

The pattern of levels then looks like this as it descends into greater detail.

(a)	1			
(b)		2		
(c)			3	
(d)				4
(e)				4 *(Notice the coordinating conjunction, 'but')*
(f)				5

Paragraph 3

Based upon a coordinate sequence model:

(a) Because of the boom–bust syndrome, property is quite an 'illiquid' investment. *(b)* It can be difficult to sell your house or land when you want to, especially at a profit. *(c)* The sale price is never guaranteed, although you can improve the chance of making a profit by trying to buy in an area where house/land prices are rising. *(d)* Even the profit may prove illusory. *(e)* You have to deduct buying and selling costs (which include legal fees, stamp duty, etc.), plus the money spent on maintenance and repair.

GAIL SEEKAMP[20]

The pattern of levels then looks like this as it enumerates property illiquidity. Only at the end does it step into a more specific statement.

(a) 1 property 'illiquid' investment
(b)   2 difficult to sell
(c)   2 sale price not guaranteed
(d)   2 profit illusory
(e)   3 deductions

Paragraph 4
A mixed sequence paragraph can return to a level No. 1 statement
at its very end. The paragraph below starts speaking about competition
policy in the European Union at the beginning, goes into articles
within the Treaty of Rome, and finally circles back to competition
policy again. I have italicised links in the sequence.

> (a) The Treaty of Rome (1957) lays down the basis for
> creating a common market and free trade between member
> states, and *competition policy* was spelt out in Articles 85 and 86
> of the Treaty. (b) European *competition policy* is crucial to the
> development of the European Union in that it helps to main-
> tain or establish a genuine *competitive structure*. (c) The thrust of
> *Article 85* is to prohibit agreements or concerted practices
> between enterprises that prevent, restrict or distort *competition*.
> (d) *Article 86* is aimed at curbing the *abusive behaviour* of
> monopolies. (e) *Regulation 17* of the Article deals with the
> registration of mergers and acquisitions. (f) *Competition policy*
> has had a major effect on many areas of European and Irish
> industry – in particular the airline industry, telecommuni-
> cations and energy.

JOHN J. LYNCH AND FRANK W. ROCHE[21]

The pattern of levels:
(a) 1
(b)   2
(c)   3
(d)   3
(e)   4
(f) 1

Paragraph 5
The following mixed sequence paragraph, again borrowed from
Benson's study,[22] presents a list of characters in coordinate sequence.
Yet in good subordinate style and with very clear control, it also
tells a bit about each one.

> (a) If you have never made yeast bread, behold one of the
> great dramas of the kitchen. (b) Every ingredient is a character.
> (c) Yeast is the prima donna. (d) Her volatile temperament is
> capable of exploitation only within given limits of heat – and
> does she resent a drafty dressing room! (e) Wheat flour is the

hero. *(f)* He has a certain secret something that makes his personality elastic and gives convincing body to his performance. *(g)* Rice, rye, corn, soy – no other flour can touch him for texture, but he is willing to share the stage with others – if they give him the lime light. *(h)* Water, milk or other liquid ingredients are the intriguers. *(i)* Any one of them lends steam to the show. *(j)* As for salt and sugar, they make essential but brief entrances; too much of either inhibits the range of the other actors. *(k)* Fat you can enlist or leave. *(l)* Use him to endow your performance with more tender and more lasting appeal. *(m)* There are quite a few extras, too, which you can ring in to give depth and variety. *(n)* Allow some ad-libbing with nuts and raisins, herbs and sprouts.

IRMA ROMBAUER[23]

(a)	1			
(b)		2		
(c)			3	
(d)				4
(e)			3	
(f)				4
(g)					5
(h)		3		
(i)				4
(j)		3		
(k)		3		
(l)				4
(m)		3		
(n)				4

Paragraph 6

The historian Paul Johnson writes a review of another historian's work. Notice how he alternates between a short sentence and a more extended sentence structure to establish a voice.

(a) Martin Gilbert is the most prodigious author of our time. *(b)* So far he has produced 48 books, some of huge size. *(c)* It is true that ten are collections of documents, rather than narratives written by him. *(d)* But even they have required industrious compilation and careful editing, and plainly involved a lot of hard work. *(e)* There is nothing hurried or sloppy about

Gilbert either. *(f)* He is always accurate and thorough. *(g)* In short, he is a phenomenon, who arouses envy among less productive professional historians. *(h)* They retaliate by saying he rarely expresses an opinion or takes up a position, that he is just a presenter rather than an analyst. *(i)* To which I reply: maybe so, but then we need a Gilbert. *(j)* He is actually a more useful historian than many analytical ones because he tackles weighty subjects, and quarries and arranges masses of material that all the rest of us can use. *(k)* He is the nearest modern approach to the best kind of medieval chronicler, such as Matthew Paris or Jean Froissart – and where would we be without them?

PAUL JOHNSON[24]

(a)	1		
(b)		2	
(c)			3
(d)				4
(e)	1		
(f)		2	
(g)	1		
(h)		2	
(i)			3
(j)			3
(k)			3

Paragraph 7

It is not always easy to chart the levels of sentences in a paragraph sequence, nor should it be; argument can rightly erupt. Furthermore, writing cannot thrive if it is always constrained by a diagnostic scheme just as a frog enjoys no improvement of life through dissection. This introductory paragraph by Augustine Martin defies charting and yet is both coherent and eloquent. I will make two attempts to chart it and finally remain unsatisfied.

(a) The fourteen lectures that comprise this book attempt to define and evaluate that great body of imaginative prose writing that has come out of Ireland in this century. *(b)* Comprehensiveness was impossible within the space available, but a determined attempt has been made to deal with what is genuinely significant in the various *genres* while pointing towards those

areas of achievement or promise which were impossible to accommodate within the central emphasis of each chapter. *(c)* Each contributor is an expert within his field, but even the most authoritative judgments are to some degree subjective, especially in the highly subjective regions of literature. *(d)* The book offers itself in terms of lively and informed opinion, rather than in any spirit of dogma. *(e)* If the views and discriminations offered prove in some cases controversial so much the better. *(f)* The object of all good criticism is to stimulate, even provoke discussion of what the creative artist has engendered.

AUGUSTINE MARTIN[25]

(a) 1				*(a)* 1		
(b)	2			*(b)*	2	
(c)	2		*or*	*(c)*	2	
(d)		3		*(d)*		3
(e)			4	*(e)*		3
(f)				5	*(f)* 1	

Paragraph 8
The next is a fine example of a mixed sequence paragraph written by Colbert Kearney in the book which Martin introduces, *The Genius of Irish Prose*. Notice how he descends into more particular exposition and still uses the list technique.

(a) The history of short fiction in Ireland parallels that of mainland Europe. *(b)* The folktale has always been an important ingredient. *(c)* So too has been the desire to explore and explain the charm and squalor of low life in town and countryside. *(d)* Early in the nineteenth century Thomas Crofton Croker had a huge success with an anthology of folklore which he called *Fairy Legends and Traditions of the South of Ireland*. *(e)* His even more interesting contemporary was William Carleton, whose career epitomises many of the conflicts which unbalanced Irish cultural life in the nineteenth century. *(f)* The heir to an oral Gaelic tradition, he became a considerable writer in English. *(g)* At one time destined for the Catholic priesthood, some of his best work was intended as an exposure of the evil influence of the Catholic clergy in Ireland. *(h)* He aspired to write novels in the English manner but his reputation rests on shorter works which are closer to storytelling in the Irish mode. *(i)* In

Traits and Stories of the Irish Peasantry Carleton, the sophisticated narrator, invites the reader into the obscurity of the Irish cabin consciousness, a consciousness which Carleton understood only too well for his own comfort. *(j)* Happily, his delight in the crazier colours of character and language subverted his didactic zeal and he created a world of exuberant and squalid innocence which retains its power to charm and chill the modern reader.

COLBERT KEARNEY[26]

(a)	1				
(b)		2			
(c)		2			
(d)			3		
(e)			3		
(f)				4	
(g)					5
(h)				4	
(i)					5
(j)						6

Paragraph 9

Patrick Sheeran employs the coordinate sequence list in his essay on Irish tradition, yet he develops some of his points to produce a mixed sequence based upon a coordinate sequence.

(a) The question of tradition in Ireland is extremely fraught, in large part because it borders on the related problem of identity. *(b)* Rather like those cosmologies which divided early Celtic Ireland into two, five or seven parts, the modern Irish tradition has been charted in terms of various typologies. *(c)* In one version Gaelic Ireland is pitted against Anglo-Irish Ireland in the rôles of colonised and coloniser. *(d)* In another both together enter an uneasy alliance to face a third, menacing English presence. *(e)* More recently, events have taught us to recognise and to add to our conceptual map a Presbyterian culture in the north of the island. *(f)* The most comprehensive – and therefore controversial – delineation of the multiple strains within our culture has been that of F.S.L. Lyons in a study with a revealing title: *Culture and Anarchy in Ireland 1890–1939*. *(g)* Here it is claimed that 'the key to the Irish problem in its modern form was the competitive coexistence with Ireland, not just of a

simple dualism between native and settler, but of a complex of
Irish and Anglo-Irish cultures operating within, and powerfully
affected by, the dominant English culture' [Lyons, 1979, 26].
(h) To complicate matters even further, disillusion with the
present state of affairs – economic, political, social – has led
others to claim that the Irish today have inherited neither the
Gaelic, Anglo-Irish nor English cultural traditions but a barren
residue of all three. *(i)* Indeed, there is a comprehensive emotional definition of Irish culture, partly stemming from James
Joyce, which sees it as a repository of speech, gesture and
ritual characterised by a sense of dispossession, grievance and
paralysis. *(j)* An extreme view would hold that the Irish
tradition hardly exists: 'Ireland is a nothing – a no-thing – an
interesting nothing, to be sure, composed of colourful parts, a
nothing-mosaic'. *(k)* This point of view is worth pursuing if
only because it is in line with a number of recent assertions
that the Irish tradition is something we have yet to create.

PATRICK SHEERAN[27]

(a) 1
(b) 1
(c) 2
(d) 2
(e) 2
(f) 2
(g)   3
(h) 2
(i)   3
(j) 2
(k)   3

Paragraph 10

Declan Kiberd balances two alternatives and thus, on the surface,
seems to work with a coordinate sequence, yet the paragraph
fundamentally moves from a theoretical position to a point of
decisive action by taking a few steps down in this mixed sequence
based upon a subordinate sequence.

(a) In theory, two kinds of freedom were available to the Irish:
the return to a past, pre-colonial Gaelic identity, still yearning
for expression if long-denied, or the reconstruction of a
national identity, beginning from first principles all over again.

(b) The first discounted much that had happened, for good as well as ill, during the centuries of occupation; the second was even more exacting, since it urged people to ignore other aspects of their past too. *(c)* The first eventually took the form of nationalism, as sponsored by Michael Collins, Éamon de Valera and the political élites; the second offered liberation, and was largely the invention of writers and artists who attempted, in Santayana's phrase, 'to make us citizens by anticipation in the world that we crave'. *(d)* The nationalism of the politicians enjoyed intermittent support from a major artist such as W.B. Yeats, but eventually he grew tired of it; the liberation preached by the artists sometimes won the loyalty of the more imaginative political figures, such as Liam Mellows or Hanna Sheehy-Skeffington. *(e)* Inevitably, neither model was sufficient unto itself: even its stoutest defenders were compelled by the brute facts of history to 'borrow' some elements of the alternative version.

DECLAN KIBERD[28]

1 *(a)* In theory, two kinds of freedom were available to the Irish: the return to a past, pre-colonial Gaelic identity, still yearning for expression if long-denied, or the reconstruction of a national identity, beginning from first principles all over again.

2 *(b)* The first discounted much that had happened, for good as well as ill, during the centuries of occupation; the second was even more exacting, since it urged people to ignore other aspects of their past too.

2 *(c)* The first eventually took the form of nationalism, as sponsored by Michael Collins, Éamon de Valera and the political elites; the second offered liberation, and was largely the invention of writers and artists who attempted, in Santayana's phrase, 'to make us citizens by anticipation in the world that we crave'.

3 *(d)* The nationalism of the politicians enjoyed intermittent support from a major artist such as W.B. Yeats, but eventually he grew tired of it; the liberation preached by the artists sometimes won the loyalty of the more imaginative political figures, such as Liam Mellows or Hanna Sheehy-Skeffington.

4 *(e)* Inevitably, neither model was sufficient unto itself: even its stoutest defenders were compelled by the

brute facts of history to 'borrow' some elements of the alternative version.

Paragraph 11

Terence Brown demonstrates the return to a more general level (c, f) in this paragraph about Irish revivalists.

(a) It is indeed with Irish public opinion, with the attitudes of the people, that the Irish revivalists are forced to contend. *(b)* In the White Paper of 1965, which followed from the *Commission on the Restoration of the Irish Language Final Report,* it is evident that the government recognized this fact. *(c)* The White Paper proposed as government policy for the forthcoming decade a number of vaguely defined objectives ('extending the use of Irish as a living language, oral and written', for example) but accepted, in a crucial sentence, that 'competent knowledge of English will be needed even in a predominantly Irish-speaking Ireland'. *(d)* Bilingualism not linguistic exchange became the new aspiration. *(e)* Nor, apparently, should that desideratum be too strenuously pursued. *(f)* While ready to agree with the Commissioner's general sentiments, the White Paper showed that the government was less prepared to move swiftly to adopt its recommendation on the gaelicization of a variety of Irish institutions. *(g)* Phrases and terms such as 'will recommend', 'will encourage', 'desirable', and 'target' suggest a governmental caution and ambiguity almost amounting to equivocation, caught as it was between a set of proposals based on little statistical and empirical research and its own sense of public opinion.

TERENCE BROWN[29]

(a)	1		
(b)		2	
(c)			3
(d)				4
(e)				4
(f)			3
(g)				4

Paragraph 12

What about a long paragraph that handles a complex topic and has abundant information, different points of view, and quotations? Can we trace a sequence or does the scheme break down in the face of abundance? Anthony Roche handles the multiple considerations of Brian Friel's artistic transition from short story writing to play writing in a series of paragraphs. One paragraph in particular addresses the issue of influences and their constrictions, and it stays within the confines of that issue. That is the paragraph's defined ground even as it explores different points of view that superficially seem to run afield. Actually the paragraph is perfectly consistent with its own topic. Notice that it provides a summary sentence and then a transitional sentence at the end.

> *(a)* Friel's move into full-time writing marked also his greater and absolute move away from prose fiction into the medium of drama. *(b)* Richard Pine concludes that Friel grew frustrated by the limitations of the *New Yorker* format: 'Triteness, encouraged by the *New Yorker* formula, is also a reason for Friel's eventual dissatisfaction with the limiting conventions of the short story.' *(c)* But there was a short story formula closer to home which Friel has cited as the shadow from which he wished to emerge, that cast by the formidable cultural presences in the 1950s of Sean O'Faolain and Frank O'Connor: *(d)* 'I was very much under the influence, as everyone at the time was, of O'Faolain and O'Connor, particularly. *(e)* O'Connor dominated our lives. *(f)* I suppose they [Friel's short stories] were really some kind of imitation of O'Connor's work.' *(g)* One potent myth which O'Connor and O'Faolain had worked hard to disseminate, as a means of culturally bolstering their own practice, was the idea that Irish writers had a particular affinity with the short story, and that this in some sense mirrored the shape and nature of the society, fragmented and destabilised. *(h)* The theory was used most of all to oppose the notion that the Irish could or should write novels, since they lacked the stable, hierarchical society that most of the classic English novels of the nineteenth century had been built around. *(i)* Such a radical theory, however, served a conventional notion of the short story. *(j)* O'Connor's influence as cited by Friel may well account in part for what George O'Brien remarks about the short stories, the singular lack of development displayed across the two volumes: *(k)* 'There is little sense of development in Friel's story-writing. *(l)* He came to his world and its themes early and, rather uncritically, remained with them until committing himself completely to the theatre.'

(m) The stories, in this respect especially, stand in opposition to the plays. *(n)* The latter are marked throughout Friel's career by a continuing pressure of formal experimentation and development. *(o)* This development is not necessarily linear; rather, it is the case with each play that Friel is responding to and writing himself out of the limitations he has inadvertently come up against in the previous one. *(p)* Put in broader cultural terms, Ireland at the close of the 1950s did not need one more short story writer, even one as accomplished as Brian Friel. *(q)* It stood in much greater need of a playwright to take the measure of and to find forms adequate to a society undergoing a profound transition.

ANTHONY ROCHE[30]

(a)	1			
(b)		2		
(c)		2		
(d)			3	
(e)				4
(f)					5
(g)			3	
(h)				4
(i)					5
(j)			3	
(k)				4
(l)					5
(m)		2		
(n)			3	
(o)				4
(p)	1 *(summary point)*			
(q)		2 *(transition sentence)*		

While the scheme I derive from Roche's paragraph may be challenged at some points, it nevertheless does trace a sequence. That said, I must reiterate that writers do not think, 'I will write a coordinate sequence paragraph here, followed by two mixed sequences, a subordinate, and then another concluding coordinate sequence'; nor, in practice, do writers consider such mapping exercises at all. Yet writers do watch the sentences in their paragraphs very carefully so that they stay linked together and do not veer away from the topic and get lost.

This mapping technique, thanks to Francis Christensen, helps us to study the structure of writers' paragraphs after they are written; it helps us to see the logic and direction of their growth. Traditionally writers learned their craft by imitating other writers. Thus, the three kinds of paragraph sequence structure assist us in better seeing how professional paragraphs are built and leave us with models to imitate. The question which must follow such an examination asks whether this idea of the three kinds of paragraph sequence extends into essay organisation. We shall turn to this consideration following a few exercises.

Exercise 1   *Paragraph Exercise*

Chart the levels in this paragraph.

(a) It was the narrow harbour, made secure by the generous bay and the sweep of the mountains that from the first attracted invaders. *(b)* In the ninth century came Norse-speaking raiders from Norway, the Vikings. *(c)* Theirs were the first long ships to come 'sniffing up the Liffey' (as a modern Irish poet puts it), ten days' hard sailing from bases in Bergen or Oslo. *(d)* Apparently these Vikings found some kind of earlier settlements of wooden huts built by the Irish along the estuary: one at a Hurdle Ford (Ath Cliath) and the other at the Black Pool (Linn Dubh). *(e)* Strung out on the coast either side of the Liffey were early Christian churches and monasteries, built and rebuilt in the previous three centuries, in the intervals between the fighting among local Irish chieftains. *(f)* Their graveyards were punctuated with the high crosses and round towers that were a Celtic specialty. *(g)* The Norwegians' specialty was a long ship and a battle-axe. *(h)* For half a century they behaved like pirates, harrying the coastal plain from their lair beside the Liffey, looting for slaves and cattle, hunting for Irish souvenirs before burning the churches.

THOMAS PAKENHAM[31]

(a)	*(e)*
(b)	*(f)*
(c)	*(g)*
(d)	*(h)*

Exercise 2   *Mixed sequence paragraph*

Write a mixed sequence paragraph that begins with the topic sentence.

I am _____.

(picky, paranoid, over-confident, pushy, patient, impatient, tolerant, intolerant, or your choice)

Exercise 3   *Paragraph exercise*

Develop this paragraph by adding sentences at lower levels. Down how many steps can you carry it?

People spend a great deal of money to maintain appearances in our culture. For instance, consider all the money people spend on clothes and cosmetics. . . .

And consider the reasons for buying an impressive car. . . .

10. Essay Organisation

In chapter 2, The Writing Process, pp. 5–7, I described the steps one takes in composing an essay. Now I shall address the structure of an essay in light of the general principle of organisation. As a sentence has a core plus additions and a paragraph has a topic sentence plus development sentences, so an essay has a thesis assertion which is developed by the topic sentences which ensue. In an essay a writer defines a subject by making an assertion about it in the introductory thesis statement, then from that assertion derives a series of main points in topic sentences and then supports each point with argument, information, or direct quotation in a series of sentences. The topic sentences can be set in a sequence of coordinate levels, in a sequence of subordinate levels, or, as is most practised, in mixed level sequence. In the coordinate sequence every topic sentence derives directly from the thesis statement. In a subordinate sequence, however, a topic sentence often grows out of an element near to the end of a previous paragraph, and not necessarily out of the previous topic sentence, although it may. It is linked much as a chain link connects at one end to the link before it and, of course, at its other end around the near end of the following link.

Before looking at paragraph sequencing, however, we should look at how a general subject is shaped into a thesis statement. Let's say you have been asked to write an essay on this topic:

> The success or failure of discipline in the home depends upon the skill of the parent(s). Discuss

To generate thought on this subject, you need to explore its key words, especially 'discipline'. Write 'success/failure–discipline–skill' in the middle of a sheet of paper, circle it and then let your mind explore those words. Around them, write down every phrase that comes to mind, draw a circle around each and a line from it to the centre circle. This is commonly known as 'brainstorming' and 'mapping' or 'ballooning'. It allows you to constellate thoughts around a central idea without linear constriction. As you proceed, you will discover several facets of the subject and then patterns of association. Probably you have studied the subject in a course, so the essay assignment is based upon lectures and texts. Thus, you will have ideas and information at hand. Let's say that you prefer 'success' in this exploration, that you see discipline finally as a positive term, that 'self-esteem' and 'logical consequences' have emerged from the many associations you have clustered around the general subject. You begin to see a logical pattern emerging.

At this point you need to make an assertion which arises from your mapping, an assertion that both defines and directs your essay; you write a thesis statement. You might even continue composing a sustained prose statement which will be your introduction. From your first 'brainstorm' you might form this statement:

> Parents who employ logical consequences as a method of discipline instil in their children self-esteem and a sense of responsibility.

This is a thesis statement. It limits the general subject, yet it is broad enough to be developed. Its terms need explanation and it requires supporting documentation and argument.

Next, topics need to emerge from the thesis statement, so another mapping exercise around key words may prove useful. Obviously 'logical consequences' need defining, replete with illustrations either hypothetical or actual. The application or 'method' needs attention. The term 'instil' must be clarified. And you will need to portray 'responsibility' and 'self-esteem' in an actual child or children so that the reader sees what you intend. These are all points or topics which stem from the thesis statement. Each one, a topic sentence, in turn will develop into paragraphs full of particular points of information and argument just as the general subject had been formed into a thesis statement and the thesis statement constelled into topic sentences.

The stages of development proceed thus:

> General subject – emerging pattern – thesis statement – topic statements – development sentences.

Once you have mapped this much material, you next organise topics into sequential order. At one time student writers were taught the 'five-paragraph' essay form. It is actually a coordinate sequence essay whose first paragraph introduces the subject and makes an assertion in the thesis statement. Three paragraphs follow, each headed by a topic sentence that derives directly from the thesis statement: points one, two, three. The essay concludes with a restatement of the thesis, empowered by the points in the argument, perhaps carrying a persuasive punch. It has been compared to musical sonata form – ABA – and writers have been exhorted to use the structure to 'tell them what you are going to tell them, tell them, and then tell them what you told them'. This sounds facetious, yet it clarifies in rough form what an essay does. Such a structure provides a very clear format and is especially useful in a timed essay examination, when the writer is put under pressure to produce an essay quickly.

While the idea of the coordinate sequence essay sounds simple, in the hands of a skilled writer it can appear rich and complex. A classic example of this structure, E.M. Forster's 'My Wood' develops the five-paragraph essay into a gem. The thesis statement, topic sentences, and barest portion of the conclusion have been set in italics. Following the essay, I will reproduce these parts in sequence to see how they proceed.

My Wood

A few years ago I wrote a book which dealt in part with the difficulties of the English in India. Feeling that they would have had no difficulties in India themselves, the Americans read the book freely. The more they read it the better it made them feel, and a cheque to the author was the result. I bought a wood with the cheque. It is not a large wood – it contains scarcely any trees, and it is intersected, blast it, by a public footpath. Still, it is the first property that I have owned, so it is right that other people should participate in my shame, and should ask themselves, in accents that will vary in horror, this very important question: *What is the effect of property upon the character?* Don't let's touch economics; the effect of private ownership upon the community as a whole is another question – a more important question, perhaps, but another one. Let's keep to psychology. *If you own things, what's their effect on you? What's the effect on me of my wood?*

In the first place, it makes me feel heavy. Property does have this effect. Property produces men of weight, and it was a man of weight who failed to get into the Kingdom of Heaven. He was not wicked, that unfortunate millionaire in the parable, he was only stout; he stuck out in front, not to mention behind, and as he wedged himself this way and that in the crystalline entrance and bruised his well-fed flanks, he saw beneath him a comparatively slim camel passing through the eye of a needle and being woven into the robe of God. The Gospels all through couple stoutness and slowness. They point out what is perfectly obvious, yet seldom realized: that if you have a lot of things you cannot move about a lot, that furniture requires dusting, dusters require servants, servants require insurance stamps, and the whole tangle of them makes you think twice before you accept an invitation to dinner or go for a bathe in the Jordan. Sometimes the Gospels proceed further and say with Tolstoy that property is sinful; they approach the difficult ground of asceticism here, where I cannot follow them. But as to the immediate effects of property on people, they just show straightforward logic. It produces men of weight. Men of weight cannot, by definition, move like the lightning from the East unto the West, and the ascent of a fourteen-stone bishop into a pulpit is thus the exact antithesis of the coming of the Son of Man. My wood makes me *feel heavy.*

In the second place, it makes me feel it ought to be larger.

The other day I heard a twig snap in it. I was annoyed at first, for I thought that someone was blackberrying, and depreciating the value of the undergrowth. On coming nearer, I saw it was not a man who had trodden on the twig and snapped it, but a bird, and I felt pleased. My bird. The bird was not equally pleased. Ignoring the relation between us, it took fright as soon as it saw the shape of my face, and flew straight over the boundary hedge into a field, the property of Mrs. Henessy, where it sat down with a loud squawk. It had become Mrs. Henessy's bird. Something seemed grossly amiss here, something that would not have occurred had the wood been larger. I could not afford to buy Mrs. Henessy out, I dared not murder her, and limitations of this sort beset me on every side. Ahab did not want that vineyard – he only needed it to round off his property, preparatory to plotting a new curve – and all the land around my wood has become necessary to me in order to round off the wood. A boundary protects. But – poor little thing – the boundary ought in its turn to be protected. Noises on the edge of it. Children throw stones. A little more, and then a little more, until we reach the sea. Happy Canute! Happier Alexander! And after all, why should even the world be the limit of possession? A rocket containing a Union Jack, will, it is hoped, be shortly fired at the moon. Mars. Sirius. Beyond which . . . But these immensities ended by saddening me. I could not suppose that my wood was the destined nucleus of universal dominion – it is so very small and contains no mineral wealth beyond the blackberries. Nor was I comforted when Mrs. Henessy's bird took alarm for the second time and flew clean away from us all, under the belief that it belonged to itself.

In the third place, property makes its owner feel that he ought to do something to it. Yet he isn't sure what. A restlessness comes over him, a vague sense that he has a personality to express – the same sense which, without any vagueness, leads the artist to an act of creation. Sometimes I think I will cut down such trees as remain in the wood, at other times I want to fill up the gaps between them with new trees. Both impulses are pretentious and empty. They are not honest movements towards money-making or beauty. They spring from a foolish desire to express myself and from an inability to enjoy what I have got. Creation, property, enjoyment form a sinister trinity in the human mind. Creation and enjoyment are both very, very good, yet they are often unattainable without a material basis, and at such moments property pushes itself in as a substitute, saying, 'Accept me instead – I'm good enough for all three.' It is not enough. It is, as Shakespeare said of lust, 'The expense of spirit in a waste of shame'; it is 'Before, a joy proposed; behind, a dream.' Yet we don't know how to shun it. It is forced on us by our economic system as the alternative to starvation. It is also forced on us by an internal defect in the soul, by the feeling that in property may lie the germs of self-development and of exquisite or heroic deeds. Our life on earth is, and ought to be, material and carnal. But we have not yet learned to manage our materialism and carnality properly; they are still entangled with the desire for ownership, where (in the words of Dante) 'Possession is one with loss.'

And this brings us to our fourth and final point: the blackberries.

Blackberries are not plentiful in this meagre grove, but they are easily seen from the public footpath which traverses it, and all too easily gathered. Foxgloves, too – people will pull up the foxgloves, and ladies of an educational tendency even grub for toadstools to show them on the Monday in class. Other ladies, less educated, roll down the bracken in the arms of their gentlemen friends. There is paper, there are tins. Pray, does my wood belong to me or doesn't it? And, if it does, should I not own it best by allowing no one else to walk there? There is a wood near Lyme Regis, also cursed by a public footpath, where the owner has not hesitated on this point. He has built high stone walls each side of the path, and has spanned it by bridges, so that the public circulate like termites while he gorges on the blackberries unseen. He really does own his wood, this able chap. Dives in Hell did pretty well, but the gulf dividing him from Lazarus could be traversed by vision, and nothing traverses it here. *And perhaps I shall come to this in time. I shall wall in and fence out until I really taste the sweets of property.* Enormously stout, endlessly avaricious, pseudocreative, intensely selfish, I shall weave upon my forehead the quadruple crown of possession until those nasty Bolshies come and take it off again and thrust me aside into the outer darkness.

E.M.FORSTER[32]

Forster achieves much of his effect through self-mockery and irony. Yet the structure is simple. We can chart the essay by marking the thesis statement, 1–Th, and the conclusion, 1–C, and the topic sentences of the main body paragraphs, 2.

1–Th What is the effect of property upon the character? . . . If you own things, what's their effect on you? What's the effect on me of my wood?

2 In the first place, it makes me feel heavy.

2 In the second place, it makes me feel it ought to be larger.

2 In the third place, property makes its owner feel that he ought to do something to it. Yet he isn't sure what. (These two sentences are coordinate with each other.)

2 And this brings us to our fourth and final point: the blackberries.

1–C And perhaps I shall come to this in time. I shall wall in and fence out until I really taste the sweets of property.

Satisfied that an essay can be organised in coordinate sequence, we ask whether it is possible for an essay to progress in a subordinate sequence. Can each topic sentence pick up a point from the previous paragraph and carry it into further specificity, much as the sentences in a subordinate sequence paragraph do? Can this type of progression be sustained? I think it can be sustained and hope to show an essay doing just so. It must be said, however, that the subordinate relationship between a subordinate clause and an independent clause in a sentence does not hold in a subordinate sequence essay. In an essay, an early paragraph is not dominant over succeeding paragraphs but generative, so the 'subordinate' paragraph depends upon the previous paragraph merely for its entrance. In this essay about Georgia O'Keeffe by Joan Didion, I highlight topic sentences in italics and the links which join them. Didion initially circles around the thesis statement in a thoughtful anecdotal fashion before she delivers it neatly in italics: *'Style is character'*.

Georgia O'Keeffe

'Where I was born and where and how I have lived is unimportant', *Georgia O'Keeffe told us* in the book of paintings and words published in her ninetieth year on earth. She seemed to be advising us to forget the beautiful face in the Stieglitz photographs. She appeared to be dismissing the rather condescending romance that had attached to her by then, the romance of extreme good looks and advanced age and deliberate isolation. 'It is what I have done with where I have been that should be of interest.' I recall an August afternoon in Chicago in 1973 when I took *my daughter*, then seven, to see what Georgia O'Keeffe had done with where she had been. One of the vast O'Keeffe 'Sky Above Clouds' canvases floated over the back stairs in the Chicago Art Institute that day, dominating what seemed to be several stories of empty light, and my daughter looked at it once, ran to the landing, and kept on looking. 'Who drew it', she whispered after a while. I told her. *'I need to talk to her',* she said finally.

My daughter was making, that day in Chicago, an entirely unconscious but quite basic *assumption about people and the work they do.* She was assuming that the glory she saw in the work reflected a glory in its maker, that the painting was the painter as the poem is the poet, that every choice one made alone –

every word chosen or rejected, every brush stroke laid or not laid down – betrayed one's character. **Style is character** [Didion's italics]. It seemed to me that afternoon that I had rarely seen so instinctive an application of this familiar principle, and I recall being pleased not only that my daughter responded to style as character but that it was *Georgia O'Keeffe's particular style to which she responded: this was a hard woman who had imposed her 192 square feet of clouds on Chicago.*

'Hardness' has not been in our century a quality much admired in women, nor in the past twenty years has it even been in official favour for men. When hardness surfaces in the very old we tend to transform it into 'crustiness' or eccentricity, some tonic pepperiness to be indulged at a distance. On the evidence of her work and what she has said about it, Georgia O'Keeffe is neither 'crusty' nor eccentric. *She is simply hard, a straight shooter, a woman clean of received wisdom and open to what she sees.* This is a woman who could early on dismiss most of her contemporaries as 'dreamy,' and would later single out one she liked as 'a very poor painter'. (And then add, apparently by way of softening the judgement: 'I guess he wasn't a painter at all. He had no courage and I believe that to create one's own world in any of the arts takes courage.') This is a woman who in 1939 could advise her admirers that they were missing her point, that their appreciation of her famous flowers was merely sentimental. 'When I paint a red hill', she observed coolly in the catalogue for an exhibition that year, 'you say it is too bad that I don't always paint flowers. A flower touches almost everyone's heart. A red hill doesn't touch everyone's heart.' This is a woman who could describe the genesis of one of her most well-known paintings – the 'Cow's Skull: Red, White and Blue', owned by the Metropolitan – as an act of *quite deliberate and derisive orneriness.* 'I thought of *the city men* I had been seeing in the East', she wrote. '*They* talked so often of writing the Great American Novel – the Great American Play – the Great American Poetry. . . . So as I was painting my cow's head on blue I thought to myself, 'I'll make it an American painting. *They will not think it great with the red stripes down the sides – Red, White and Blue – but they will notice it.'*

The city men. The men. They [Didion's italics]. *The words crop up again and again as this astonishingly aggressive woman tells us what was on her mind when she was making her astonishingly* *aggressive paintings*. It was those city men who stood accused of sentimentalizing her flowers: 'I made you take time to look at what I saw and when you took time to really notice my flower you hung all your associations with flowers on my flower and you write about my flower as if I think and see what you think and see – and I don't.' *And I don't* [Didion's italics]. Imagine those words spoken, and the sound you hear is *don't tread on me* [Didion's italics]. 'The men' believed it impossible to paint New York, so Georgia O'Keeffe painted New York. 'The men' didn't think much of her bright colour, so she made it brighter. The men yearned toward Europe so she went to Texas, and then New Mexico. The men talked about Cézanne, 'long involved remarks about the "plastic quality" of his form and color', and took one another's long involved remarks, in the view of *this angelic rattlesnake in their midst*, altogether too seriously. 'I can paint one of those dismal-coloured paintings like the men', the woman who regarded herself always as an outsider remembers thinking one day in 1922, and she did: a painting of a shed 'all low-toned and dreary with the tree beside the door'. She called this *act of rancour* 'The Shanty' and hung it in her next show. 'The men seemed to approve of it,' she reported fifty-four years later, *her contempt undimmed. 'They seemed to think that maybe I was beginning to paint. That was my only low-toned dismal-coloured painting.'*

  Some women fight and others do not. Like so many successful guerrillas in the war between the sexes, *Georgia O'Keeffe seems to have been equipped early with an immutable sense of who she was and a fairly clear understanding that she would be required to prove it.* On the surface her upbringing was conventional. She was a child on the Wisconsin prairie who played with china dolls and painted watercolours with cloudy skies because sunlight was too hard to paint and, with her brother and sisters, listened every night to her mother read stories of the Wild West, of Texas, of Kit Carson and Billy the Kid. *She told adults* that she wanted to be an artist and was embarrassed when they asked what kind of artist she wanted to be: she had no idea 'what kind.' She had no idea what artists did. She had never seen a picture that interested her, other than a pen-and-ink Maid of Athens in one of her mother's books, some Mother Goose illustrations printed on cloth, a tablet cover that showed a little girl with pink roses, and the painting of Arabs on horseback that hung in her grandmother's parlour. At thirteen, in a Dominican convent, she was mortified when *the sister corrected her drawing*. At Chatham Episcopal Institute in Virginia she painted lilacs and sneaked time alone to walk out to where she could see the line of the Blue Ridge Mountains on the horizon. At the Art Institute in Chicago she was shocked by the presence of live models and wanted to abandon anatomy lessons. At the Art Students League in New York one of her fellow students *advised her* that, since he would be a great painter and she would end up teaching painting in a girls' school, any work of hers was less important than modeling for him. Another *painted over her work to show her* how the Impressionists did trees. *She had not before heard how the Impressionists did trees and she did not much care.*

At twenty-four she left all those opinions behind and went for the first time to live in Texas, where there were no trees to paint and no one to tell her how not to paint them. In Texas there was only the horizon she craved. In Texas she had her sister Claudia with her for a while, and in the late afternoons they would walk away from town and toward the horizon and watch the *evening star* come out. 'That evening star fascinated me', she wrote. 'It was in some way very exciting to me. My sister had a gun, and as we walked she would throw bottles into the air and shoot as many as she could before they hit the ground. *I had nothing but to walk into nowhere and the wide sunset space with the star.* Ten watercolours were made from that star.' In a way one's interest is compelled as much by the sister Claudia with the gun as by the painter Georgia with the star, but only the painter left us this shining record. Ten watercolours were made from *that star.*

JOAN DIDION[33]

Didion writes what is commonly known as the 'occasional essay'. It is not an academic mode but like academic writing it is expository as it unfolds a subject, step by step, link by link in a subordinate sequence. On the surface the occasional essay seems pedestrian. Yet from such pieces as this, we see the craft shine from every sentence and considered link.

No externally imposed schematic reading can completely fit every essay because an essay is the shape of living thought. Still, it helps to study essays for the structural links and to think about such links as we write ourselves. The task of application becomes even more difficult when we try to apply the mixed sequence scheme to a longer, complex, academic essay. Here I reproduce only the first section of an essay on 'A Changing Society: Ireland Since the 1960s'. This section of the essay, subtitled 'Economic Growth and Integration: The Irish Economies Post 1958', itself has two parts: one on the Republic of Ireland and the other on Northern Ireland. Each part begins at level 1. I reproduce only the introductory thesis statement and all of the topic sentences. I attempt to number each as I perceive it is linked to a level above it. (Level charting is always debatable around complex texts.) And I highlight some linking words where they appear. While this exercise does not do justice to the essay, it may honour its structural coherence.

From 'A Changing Society: Ireland Since the 1960s'.

1- Intro: If post-independence Ireland can be characterised as insular and conservative, preoccupied with stability rather than progress, then the 1960s may be said to have witnessed *change* and a certain liberalisation in Irish society.

1 The trauma of the 1950s, characterised by economic stagnation and high levels of emigration, was replaced in the 1960s by an equally dramatic *change* of direction in the fortunes of the southern Irish *economy*.

2 As on previous occasions, it was the combination of a stringent critique of domestic policy in conjunction with major external developments which forced a fundamental re-orientation of *economic policy*.

3 The principal component of the *new strategy* of economic development was the need to re-orientate domestic industry away from its focus on a stagnant domestic market and to exploit the *opportunities of expanding foreign* markets.

4 *This emphasis* on the need to abandon protection and adopt trade liberalisation reflected in turn external developments.

3 Just as the main components of the *new strategy* were articulated and refined during the 1950s, so too it was during this period that the principal institutional and legislative measures, which provided the foundation for future industrial *expansion*, were implemented.

4 The formal *end to protection* was clearly signalled when Ireland, following the United Kingdom, applied for membership of the EEC in 1961.

5 *As a result* of *this re-orientation*, there were dramatic *changes* in the volume and composition of Ireland's trade.

3 While the Republic's trade dependence or 'degree of openness' greatly increased over the 1960s and '70s, the *composition of trade* also *changed* dramatically.

3 A third dimension to the *changing* economy concerned the *trading pattern* with the United Kingdom.

4 The main reasons for the *diversification* of the Republic's export markets can be quickly listed: . . . [*'diversification' picked up from last sentence in previous paragraph*]

2–3 A novel feature of Irish economic *policy* after 1958 was the introduction of a *series of 'programmes' or 'plans'* for economic expansion. . . . *The First Programme.* . . .

3 Encouraged by these results, the government launched a *Second Programme* for Economic *Expansion* to cover the years 1964–70.

4 The contribution of economic planning to the *sustained growth* of the 1960s remains unclear.

3 A *Third Programme* for Economic and Social Development was introduced in 1969 to replace the Second Programme, which had been abandoned in 1967, and this new Programme was to cover the period up to *1972*.

2–C After *1973* economic *planning* was declared inappropriate because of the increased uncertainty in the external environment, and Ireland attempted to adjust to the world of rising oil prices.

1 In Northern Ireland the 1950s and early 1960s were on balance years of *steady economic progress*.

2 The tradition of government intervention in Northern Ireland to *promote industrial development* can be traced to the 1930s, when the *policy framework* which provided for grants, interest-free loans and exemption from rates, was first established.

3 As part of its *strategy* to *revitalise* the industrial base of its economy Northern Ireland sought to attract *new foreign investment* as part of the United Kingdom economy.

3 The *reduction of unemployment* was the main *objective* of successive Northern Ireland governments, and this *aim* was central to a number of major economic plans produced during the 1960s, particularly the Wilson Plan of 1965.

1-C Since the early 1970s the intensity of the *civil unrest* has caused increasing *problems* for the Northern Ireland *economy*.

This concludes one sustained look at essay organisation. It articulates a strategy of associative thought clustered around a general subject in order to shape a thesis statement and topic sentences, and it defines three kinds of organisational sequences which essays can be formed into. I have not dealt with classical issues of the compare and contrast essay, wherein parallel structure becomes a controlling device, or the persuasive essay that might start from particular points and work up to a general impact statement, or the particularly narrative essay that uses chronology as its controlling device. Some of these ways are taken up in chapter 20, Writing a Report, pp. 139–58. Overall, it needs to be said that content will demand its right form. A writer is always searching for the right form; it's a way of thinking.

11. Adjective Clauses

When we worked with subordination in the sentence (see pp. 51–7), we joined clause to clause by means of the subordinating conjunction. Actually we were joining clause core to clause core so that a whole predication was linked to another whole predication. These subordinate clauses can be called adverb clauses.

The next type of clause we shall consider attaches itself to a noun and adds more information about that noun within the sentence. We say it modifies the noun. It modifies the noun much as an adjective 'describes' a noun. We shall name these clauses adjective clauses because they function as adjectives. In traditional grammar, they were called 'relative clauses'.

> *adjective phrase:* the *long* [report]
> *adjective clause:* [the report] *which is long*

Definition

An adjective clause is a dependent clause that modifies or describes a noun. The whole clause functions as an adjective. Here are two complete sentences, each with an adjective clause.

> I just purchased a house *which had been on the market for over a year.*
> The document *that he lost* has been found.

In order for adjective clauses to be properly joined to the nouns they describe, they need conjunctions. There are seven of them:

which	that
who	whom
whose	when
where	

The conjunction has two functions.

> 1. It renames the noun; it is a 'relative pronoun'.
> 2. It joins the adjective clause to the noun.

Demonstration

In the following examples, the adjective clauses are separated and italicised.

Example 1 – WHICH

It begins with 'which' when it refers to a noun that isn't a person; it refers to things, abstractions, and animals. It can be either the subject or an object of the verb in the adjective clause.

> My last essay, / ***which** I presented to my tutor,* / needs to be slightly rewritten.

'Which' renames 'essay'; it is the conjunction and the object of the verb 'presented'.

> I have read your essay, / ***which** contains my new theory.*

'Which' renames 'essay'; it is the conjunction and the subject of the verb 'contains'.

Example 2 – THAT

It begins with 'that' when it refers to people, things, abstractions, and animals (although many prefer 'who' for people in writing). It can be either the subject or an object of the verb in the adjective clause.

> Jameson is the man / ***that** advised me on the legal aspects of my proposal.*

'That' renames 'man'; it is the conjunction and, here, the subject of the verb 'advised'.

> That is the dog ***that*** bit me several times.

'That' renames 'dog'; it is the conjunction and the subject of the verb 'bit'.

Example 3 – WHO

An adjective clause begins with 'who' when it refers to a person, and that person is also the subject of the verb within the adjective clause.

The woman / *who boarded the plane to Paris* / mistakenly took my attaché case.

'Who' renames 'woman'; it is both the conjunction and the subject of the verb 'boarded'.

Example 4 – WHOM

It begins with 'whom' when it refers to a person, and that person is the object of a verb within the adjective clause.

My colleague, / *whom you just met,* / had an brief career as a concert pianist.

'Whom' renames 'colleague'; it is the conjunction and the object of the verb 'met':

'You just met *my colleague.*'

Or 'You just met *him*. (A memory device: the *m* of *him* echoes the *m* of *whom*.)

Or 'You just met *her*.

Example 5 – WHOSE

It begins with 'whose' when it refers to any noun that owns something. Within the adjective clause whose is a possessive pronoun like his [case], her [letter] or its [system].

I have begun work for a client / *whose business has been floundering.*

'Whose' renames 'client'; it is the conjunction and the possessive pronoun attached to the subject 'business'.

Example 6 – WHEN

It begins with 'when' if it refers to a noun of time.

We have a meeting on Thursday, / *when everyone involved in the project returns from location.*

'When' renames 'Thursday'; it is the conjunction and, within the adjective clause, the object of an unspoken prepositional phrase, 'on Thursday': Everyone returns on Thursday.

Example 7 – WHERE

It begins with 'where' if it refers to a noun of place.

> We shall meet in the restaurant, / ***where*** *we can discuss the project during dinner.*

'Where' renames 'restaurant'; it is the conjunction and the object of an unspoken prepositional phrase, 'in the restaurant': We can discuss the project during dinner in the restaurant.

Further Examples

In each the following examples, the second sentence is joined to the first one with the help of the adjective clause construction. Notice that the word italicised in the second sentence gets changed into one of the seven adjective clause conjunctions which renames the word italicised in the first sentence.

Example 1

> Let's decide upon a *day*. We can meet *then*.
> Let's decide upon a day ***when*** *we can meet.*

Example 2

> The *woman* is my aunt. *She* is standing by the entrance
> The woman ***who*** *is standing by the entrance* is my aunt.

Example 3

> The *box* contained the new computer. *It* fell off the table.
> The box, ***which*** *fell off the table*, contained the new computer.

Example 4

> This is a very interesting *plan*. You proposed *it*.
> This is a very interesting plan ***that*** *you proposed.*

Example 5

> Richard purchased a new *car*. *It* gave him endless problems.
> Richard purchased a new car ***that*** *gave him endless problems.*

Example 6

> I just met a *man*. I admire *him* greatly.
> I just met a man **whom** *I admire greatly.*

Example 7

> That is the *student*. *Her* design received all the awards
> That is the student **whose** *design received all the awards.*

Example 8

> Do you remember the *time*? We first thought of this
> concept *then*.
> Do you remember the time **when** *we first thought of this*
> *concept?*

A Comma Rule

Sometimes an adjective clause should be separated from the noun it modifies by commas and sometimes it should not. It is the *noun* which determines whether or not the clause should be set off.

If the noun is already self-defined, it needs no further definition from the adjective clause, and the clause is separated by commas; it is a 'free modifier', which really means that it is free to be removed without taking away essential meaning with it. Convention tells us to use 'which' and 'who' at the front of a free modifier rather than 'that'. Here are several typical situations in which commas are needed.

Example 1 PROPER NOUNS

> *Barbara*, who works night and day, is an excellent solicitor.
> *The Burren*, which is one huge limestone pavement,
> attracts visitors from all over the world.

Both Barbara and the Burren are already defined by their names. The adjective clause adds background information that tells the reader more but does not essentially define the noun.

Example 2 POSSESSIVE WORDS

> *Brian's computer disk*, which fell to the floor, has a system
> error.
> *My brother*, who has a way with people, calmed every-
> one's nerves during the crisis.

Example 3 NOUNS REFERRING TO ALL MEMBERS OF A CLASS
OF THINGS OR GROUP OF PEOPLE OR OTHER LIVING
CREATURES

> *Copper*, which has numerous important uses, is growing
> scarce.
> Gardeners hate *bindweed*, which grows rapidly and engulfs
> everything in its path.
> *Japanese cars*, which are very well built, have captured an
> important share of the world market. (*Cars are defined
> by 'Japanese'*.)
> Let us pity *the armadillo*, which has been abused by
> advertising.

The next two examples raise an important issue about the use of
commas.

Example 4 WHERE THE ADJECTIVE CLAUSE DOES NOT DEFINE THE
NOUN: A 'FREE MODIFIER'

As we have seen, we use a comma when the adjective clause *does
not* define the noun that includes all members of its class; it is 'free'.
In Example 5, I show the effect of removing the commas.

> *Solicitors*, who charge outrageous fees, are a disgrace.

The commas indicate that all solicitors are a disgrace.

> *The boat*, which you bought last week, has sprung a leak.

The commas tell the reader that there is only the one boat and it
has sprung a leak. The adjective clause merely provides background
information.

Example 5 WHERE THE ADJECTIVE CLAUSE DEFINES THE NOUN: 'A
BOUND MODIFIER'

If the adjective clause defines the noun, we do not use commas.
The adjective clause is essentially bound to the noun: a 'bound
modifier', which means that it cannot be removed without taking
away essential information. Convention tells us to use 'that' or
'who' when the adjective clause is bound.

> *Solicitors* who charge outrageous fees are a disgrace.

This sentence refers to only some members of the group, only the
ones who charge outrageous fees; only they are a disgrace.

The boat that you bought last week has sprung a leak.

This sentence indicates that only one boat among others that the person may own has sprung a leak, the boat that the owner bought last week.

I just met *someone* who deeply impressed me.
I want a *chocolate bar* that has a full one-eighth inch chocolate coating around it.

In each case the adjective clause *defines* the noun and, therefore, is 'bound' to it: no comma.

The Who / Whom Confusion

When the noun that an adjective clause modifies is a person, you must decide whether to use who or whom in the clause. Remember that 'who' acts as a subject and 'whom' acts as an object within the adjective clause even when they are placed at the front as conjunctions. To tell which is correct, you need to transform your adjective clause into a sentence in this way:

Sean, *who won the competition*, wore a big smile.

who won the competition   (*adjective clause* – 'who' is the subject)
He won the competition.   (*sentence* – 'who' = 'he')

The chairman, *whom Sean had always admired*, gave him the award.

whom Sean had always admired (*adjective clause* – 'whom' is the object)
Sean had always admired *him*.   (*sentence* – 'whom'='him')

Recapitulation

When the conjunction of the adjective clause functions as a *subject* (Sean/he), use who. When the conjunction of the adjective clause functions as an *object* (chairman/him), use whom.

Exercise 1   *Who or Whom?*

In the following sentences, choose between 'who' and 'whom'.

1. Mary, (*who / whom*) found an important lost document, tried to keep it a secret until the right moment.
2. John, (*who / whom*) Mary can't stand, found out about it yet had no proof she had it.
3. John came into her office with Jane, (*who / whom*) he had told about the discovery.
4. Jane, (*who / whom*) liked Mary, was both cautious and curious.
5. Mary, (*who / whom*) detected John's suspicion, ordered him from her office.
6. John, (*who / whom*) resisted her rejection, finally left.
7. Jane, (*who / whom*) Mary invited to stay, did so.
8. After Mary had confided in her, Jane told Mary that her discovery had been disclosed to John by Gerald, (*who / whom*) Mary knew was her enemy.
9. Mary fumed a great deal about nasty, calculating people, of (*who / whom*) Gerald was a perfect example.
10. Gerald, (*who / whom*) knocked and suddenly entered the room, observed the scowl on Mary's face and guessed why it was there.
11. At that point John, (*who / whom*) had gathered forces, returned with five other people, including the supervisor.
12. Mary, (*who / whom*) Jane had stepped in front of, realised that she would not be able to keep her discovery a secret any longer.
13. Dark looks were directed at her and Jane, (*who / whom*) wanted to protect her.
14. Both John and Gerald, (*who / whom*) sensed their moment of victory had come, began to disclose the secret.
15. But Mary, (*who / whom*) the supervisor had always trusted far more than either John or Gerald, stepped forward and handed the document to him.
16. She said she wanted to present it to him in private, so he could decide the best way to handle it with the client, (*who / whom*) had grown suspicious since it went missing.

Solutions are given on p. 159.

Exercise 2	*Adjective clause conjunctions*

Join these pairs of sentences into one sentence using the adjective clause conjunctions:

that   which   who   whom   whose   when   where

1. A problem is the harmful effect of car emissions on the environment. We must face this problem.
2. Cars have a particularly damaging effect. The cars are not maintained properly.
3. I have just visited a house. The owners built an enormous kitchen there.
4. The pond contains twelve different kinds of fish. They all eat the same food.
5. This tree was planted here fifty years ago. You are leaning against it.
6. My grandfather started this business. You never met him.
7. The man's hat blew off his head. The man ran in front of a bus after it.
8. We should decide upon a day. We could meet then.
9. The lake has overflowed. Thousands of people live beside it.
10. I just saw the face of a man. I think I used to know him years ago.
11. This report has been prepared for the consumer. It covers only the economic and design features of this year's models.
12. The client reigns supreme in the mind of the management. His/Her every want is taken into consideration.
13. Last year most Irish tourists travelled to Spain. Last year Spain had exceptionally hot weather.
14. We need to find the person. He/She can provide the background information on this problem.
15. A company will be awarded the contract this spring. Then all the bids will have been reviewed.

Solutions are given on p. 159.

12. Noun Clauses

- **A clause** has both a subject and a conjugated verb in it.
- **A noun clause** is a dependent clause that acts as a single noun. You know it by how it functions in a sentence. It may be

    The subject of a sentence: Whoever is happy knows the secret of life.

    The complement of a verb (predicate complement): She is *what she wants to be.*

    The direct object: He knows *that they live nearby.*

    The indirect object: He gave *whoever wanted one* a ticket.

    The object of a preposition: He showed the picture to *whoever wanted to see it.*

Noun clauses begin with a subordinating conjunction or a relative pronoun, much like those that begin adjective clauses:

1. *as a subject:*

    I did not know *who* did it.
    He told the story to *whoever* would listen.
    Whatever is worth doing at all is worth doing well.

2. *as a direct object:*

    He knows *that* he put the box somewhere.
    I did not see *whom* he struck.
    I do not know *what* he meant.
    You may have *whichever* you choose.
    I do not know *which* course he will pursue.

3. *as an object of a preposition:*
I did not see *to whom* he gave it.
We did not go *to where* we were directed.

Review

You know a noun clause by the way it *functions* as a noun in the sentence.

13. Verbal Phrases

Demonstration of Verbal Phrases

Example 1

> The usher looked at the group of children disapprovingly, *wrinkling his nose as if he had just detected a bad smell.*

Example 2

> *Removing our coats*, we climbed the stairs to the balcony.

Example 3

> The mummy of the Egyptian Pharaoh lay at the centre of the museum's main room, *guarded by two humourless curators and surrounded by a maze of guide ropes.*

Example 4

> *To complete all the tasks on the list and not forget some detail*, I kept very careful notes.

Example 5

> *Given the little information available on this subject*, I was unable to write a thorough report.

In the examples above, notice that one action is expressed in an independent clause (not italicised) while another is set beside it in a phrase (italicised), either before or after. Notice that the phrase has no subject and only an incomplete or partial verb, called a verbal, which is set in bold type. In traditional terminology it is called a 'participial verb form'.

Definition

Such a phrase that starts with a verbal and has no subject word is called a verbal phrase. Verbal phrases help a writer to show actions going on beside other actions, either leading in as does Example 2 above or continuing on as Example 1. A verbal phrase can help present steps in a procedure as does Example 4, or express a causal action which leads to another action as does Example 5.

Verbal phrases come in three forms. The most popular is the *-ing* form.

-ing form (present participle)	*to form* (infinitive)	*have form* (past participle)
walking	to walk	walked
drawing	to draw	drawn
thinking	to think	thought
taking	to take	taken

All three verbal forms join ideas, which would otherwise be contained in two sentences, into one efficient sentence. Here are examples of verbal phrases in the three forms.

Example 6

Two sentences: The police were watching a drug dealer from the window of a second-floor apartment. They photographed him making a sale.

One sentence: *Watching* a drug dealer from the window of a second-floor apartment, the police photographed him making a sale.

Example 7

Two sentences: The client was intrigued by the proposal. He nodded and smiled throughout the presentation.

One sentence: *Intrigued* by the proposal, the client nodded and smiled throughout the presentation.

Or: The client was intrigued by the proposal, *nodding* and *smiling* throughout the presentation.

Example 8

Two sentences: I wanted to finish the rough draft of my report by the morning. I stayed up half the night working on it.

One sentence: [In order] *To finish* the rough draft of my report by the morning, I stayed up half the night working on it.

An Important Feature of Verbal Phrases

Because a verbal phrase doesn't have its own subject, it needs to attach itself to one. In other words, a verbal must have an agent.

The agent of the verbal is the subject of the clause to which the verbal phrase is attached.

It is this link between the verbal and the clause subject that correctly joins the verbal phrase to the clause; this link keeps the verbal phrase from 'dangling'.

Example 9

This sentence works:

Speaking loudly, Mark delivered his speech to the attentive audience.

Who is 'speaking loudly'? Mark, of course; Mark is both the *subject* of the clause and the *agent* of the verbal phrase, 'speaking loudly'. Observe what happens when the subject doesn't work as the agent of the verbal:

Speaking loudly, the attentive audience listened to Mark's speech.

This doesn't work because we know that talking audiences don't listen attentively.

Example 10

The same rule holds when the verbal phrase comes at the end of the sentence, as here:

I walked through the forest, *observing the birds and the bees.*
(*This works because I, the subject, am doing the observing.*)

However:

> The *forest* was a pleasure to stroll through, *observing the birds and the bees.*

This doesn't work because there is no word, no agent, in the sentence to tell who is doing the observing, and the subject, 'forest', cannot be the observer.

A major cause of the dangling verbal phrase

Many times a verbal phrase is left dangling by a writer who misuses the passive voice.

Example 11

> *Poor* (passive voice): *Thinking* that they had covered all aspects of the subject, the *report* was submitted by the researchers. (*The report is not thinking.*)
>
> *Improved* (active voice): *Thinking* that they had covered all aspects of the subject, the *researchers* submitted the report.

A Comma Rule

A verbal phrase is set apart from the clause to which it is attached by a comma.

An exception

Sometimes in mid-sentence, the verbal phrase simply follows and modifies a noun that is not the subject of the main clause:

Example 12

> I walked into a room full of angry *shareholders arguing* loudly and *shaking* deeds in the air.

This is perfectly correct.

Exercise 1   *Verbal phrases*

Locate the verbal phrases in the following sentences. It is possible that a sentence contains no verbal phrase.

1. Forced to withdraw to his corner of the ring, the inflamed boxer spat out his mouth guard.

2. Having arranged everything in his backpack, Michael began the day's long tramp up the mountain.

3. To provide the entertainment, Joe rented a stereo and lighting equipment from an agency.

4. The city, clinging to its ground beside its swollen river, waited for the ferocious tropical storm to exhaust its fury.

5. Images from the space station began to appear, enhanced by computer technology.

6. Worries about utility bills, food costs, and the need of everyone for new shoes began to show on her face.

Exercise 2   *Verbal phrases*

Combine these sentences or clauses using verbal phrases.

1. You must get the car started. You must pump the accelerator twice and turn the key.

2. She decided to fly to London rather than to take the ferry and train. She rang the ticket agent.

3. The mayor was pleased by all the attention. He smiled and waved to his adoring public.

4. Car makers often seem to correct potentially dangerous defects only when forced to by government action. They apparently hope their negligence will go unnoticed.

5. You should write according to a plan, leave yourself plenty of time for revising, and proof-read your work carefully. You should do these things in order to compose a successful essay.

6. People made their way to the beach. They were burdened by striped umbrellas, canvas rafts, and coolers full of lemonade.

7. You want to get there quickly. Turn right at the second roundabout.

8. He was hoping for a winner. The man bet all his money on the race.

Exercise 3   *Verbal phrases*

Fill in the blanks with a verbal phrase, using the form suggested in brackets following each sentence.

Example: _____ , Jervis walked through the graveyard. (*-ing* form)
Solution: Whistling loudly, Jervis walked through the graveyard.

---

1. _____ , you must leave the house twenty minutes early. (*to* form)

2. _____ , the well-dressed gentleman was knocked down and robbed of his watch and wallet. (*have* form)

3. The junior minister was able to answer all of the party leader's questions, _____ . (*-ing* form)

4. _____ , ring the alarm company and give the code. (*to* form)

5. _____ , the little boy tried to hide his chocolate-covered hands. (*have* form)

6. Mary, _____ , smoked a packet of cigarettes and watched the clock. (*-ing* form)

| Exercise 4 | *Verbal phrases* |

Keeping the main clause as it is written, write three expanded sentences, one sentence with an *-ing* verbal phrase, another with a *have* verbal phrase, and a third with a *to-* verbal phrase.

1. The judge ordered the courtroom to be cleared.

    A.

    B.

    C.

2. The butler skidded on the freshly waxed floor.

    A.

    B.

    C.

3. Most people will admit to some little addiction.

    A.

    B.

    C.

Exercise 5   *Verbal phrases*

Correct these dangling verbal phrases.

1. Gasping for breath and breaking into perspiration, the bus pulled away as I ran to the stop.

2. Bored and distracted, the report was read with no enthusiasm.

3. The exam was passed by taking enough time to think about each question before answering it.

4. By avoiding complex language, the readability of insurance policies can be increased.

5. Being from a large family with six sisters and one brother, quarrels, battles, and screams of 'I hate you!' were not uncommon.

6. To analyse the budget usefully, last year's expenditures must be considered.

7. A difficult written examination must be completed in order to enter the legal profession.

8. The source of the problem can be seen now, when looking at the issue in its entirety.

9. In choosing the Olympic site, a new code of political ethics seems to have evolved by the committee.

10. Good books must be read, to write well.

14. Verbal Absolute Phrases

Formula of Verbal Absolute Phrases

Subject word + verbal:
. . . his motor running . . .
. . . her report finished . . .
. . . the award given . . .

Definition

Verbal absolute phrases are simply verbal phrases that have nouns in front of them; in other words, they have their own 'subjects' or agents, but the verb remains incomplete. These phrases allow you to show actions going on beside other actions yet enacted by different subjects. They allow you to layer a description, to build up a complex picture, to re-enact an intricate procedure. And they rescue you from composing sentences with dangling verbal phrases like this:

Problematic: *Soiled and torn*, Cinderella limped home in her old clothes while a large pumpkin rolled clumsily along beside her. (Is *she* torn, or are her *clothes*?)

Improved: *Her old clothes soiled and torn*, Cinderella limped home while a large pumpkin rolled clumsily along beside her.

Demonstration

Example 1

The roof was 300% over stressed, the *girders loaded* well beyond their limit, *panels* periodically *popping out* and *falling* to the floor below.

Example 2

The *sun shining* down the opening in his den, the badger blinked tentatively as he woke from his long winter sleep, the *blood flooding* back into long unused muscles, one hind *leg stretching* and *shaking*, his *tongue passing* twice over his dry lips and nose. The badger stirred and crawled out into the spring sunshine, a few *weeds parting* as he emerged.

Example 3

Mr Pomeroy felt particularly self-satisfied that day, his *derby cocked* jauntily to one side, his gloved *hand* fondly *working* the ivory head of his walking stick, his *spats gleaming* in the spring sunlight, the *sun* itself openly *admiring* his whole countenance. He stopped at a garden bed in the middle of the green to admire the display of spring flowers, the whole *atmosphere seeming* to stop with him, even the restless *butterflies pausing* to bask a moment in the sun, their *wings held* open, their *colours blending* perfectly with the yellows, blues, and reds of the flower petals. Yes, for a moment all creation smiled on Mr Pomeroy, and he smiled back, self-satisfied: *Mr Pomeroy satisfied* with creation.

| Exercise 1 | *Verbal absolute phrases* |

Combine these sentences by using the verbal absolute phrase.

1. His temper was rising quickly. The garda pulled the car over to the side of the road.

2. The motorist waited patiently. Her heart beat wildly. Her anxiety level was quietly yet clearly reaching psychotic heights.

3. The importance of 'pure' research has become suspect. The public's enthusiasm for nonindustrial science has started to wane.

4. His knees were shattered. The forward crawled off the pitch. His body was convulsed with pain. His head drooped. His eyes were swollen almost shut.

5. The timing is erratic. The use of dynamics is apparently arbitrary. The musicianship is atrocious. This recording of Stravinsky's *The Rite of Spring* is almost unbearable.

6. Holmes left the scene of the crime. His hat was tilted precariously on his head. His pipe was securely clamped between his teeth. His magnifying glass was tucked safely in the lower right-hand pocket of his trench coat.

| Exercise 2 | *Verbal absolute phrases* |

Expand these sentences using the verbal absolute phrase construction.

1. She pored over the report.

2. He drove onto the building site.

3. The supervisor walked onto the floor.

15. Parallel Structure

Definition of Parallel Structure

Four coordinating conjunctions – and, but, yet, or – join phrases of all kinds: subjects, verbs, objects, prepositional phrases, verbal phrases, noun and adjective phrases. In writing, those phrases must be like grammatical structures used in the same way. This is called parallel structure.

In order to see whether the structures you've joined are parallel, first look at the one that comes after the conjunction. Then look for another similar structure before the conjunction. If you find the same kinds of structures both after and before the conjunction, then your joinery is parallel. If not, then one of the structures needs to be changed so that both are parallel to each other.

Demonstration

Two subjects:	*The advertising firm* and *the client* agreed upon a package.
Two verbs:	The client *liked* the design and *signed* a contract.
Two objects:	The design team produced a *logo* and a colour *scheme* for the presentation.
Prepositional phrases:	They produced the presentation *on paper* and *in video format.*
Adjectives:	The design was both *slick* and *professional.*
Verbal phrases:	*Discussing a timetable* and *setting due dates*, the two parties finally agreed upon an overall schedule.
Noun phrases:	*A simple design* yet *an effective one*, it targets a group between the ages of 14 and 45.

Exercise 1   *Parallel structure*

Draw lines to match each structure in the first column with the same kind in the second column. (Can you name the structures?)

Examples:

in the forest

a turkey

that she had to pay the bill

that her wallet had been stolen
(*noun clauses*)

under the stars
(*prepositional phrases*)

a blueberry pie
(*noun phrases*)

---

galloping across the field	nearly four thousand people who had the injection suffered neurological damage
at the airport	clear
that nobody could save him	who always slept with a gun under his pillow
a group of school children	happily
the swine flu vaccination proved more dangerous than the flu	stepped into the room
sunny	in the morning
to fight	falling over the old stone wall
who had been mugged twice before	that he had only himself to depend on
loudly	their bright, new lunch pails
walked down the dark hall	to yell

Exercise 2   *Parallel structure*

Circle the conjunction and underline the parallel structures in the following sentences. Can you name the structures?

Examples: • The conclusions were based not <u>on hasty generalisations</u> (but) <u>on years of careful research</u>.
             • <u>Chips, burgers</u> (and) <u>cokes</u> are standard fast food fare everywhere now.

---

1. The lectures I attended were long, dry, and monotonous.

2. She didn't want to be late, so she left work early.

3. Students can be successful if they buy the assigned books, do the required reading and take careful notes.

4. Raising interest rates is a costly but necessary way of reducing inflation.

5. Wanting to trust her colleague yet remembering the times he had deceived her, she walked out of the room.

6. Either the junior minister will attend the opening and make a speech, or the director will conduct all the proceedings.

7. The architect argued that his building suited the local landscape and that his critics were wrong to say it clashed.

8. The reviewer couldn't decide whether he should ignore the awful book or write an unfavourable review.

Exercise 3	*Parallel structure*

In each of the following sentences, add to the structure (in italics) an additional *parallel* structure in the blank space.

Example: *Upset* yet _____ , the tenant told his landlord he would not pay the rent.

Possibilities: firm, polite, clear

---

1. *Teenagers* and _____ agree that they have problems communicating with one another.

2. In order to keep your body healthy, you should *sleep eight hours a night*, ___ _____ , and _____ .

3. *Intelligent* but _____ , he had a hard time getting a job.

4. *Seeing themselves as the victors* or _____ _____ , they fought stoically until the end.

5. *Arriving for work regularly* but not _____ _____ , she knew she might lose her job.

6. The ad appealed to women who *wanted to lead exciting lives* yet _____ _____ .

7. I bought a car which had an irritating habit of *breaking down frequently* or _____ _____ .

Exercise 4   *Parallel structure*

In the following sentences, underline the elements that are being joined and correct them so that they are parallel.

Example:
(*Poor*)   She was so eager to wear the dress that she tried exercise, steam baths, and was taking diet pills.

(*Improved*) She was so eager to wear the dress that she tried exercise, steam baths, and diet pills.

---

1. The good life is one inspired by love, and where knowledge is used as a guide.

2. She walked slowly, big flakes of snow falling onto her overcoat, and they clung to the hair that covered her ears.

3. After breakfast we hurry to work, but when we have finished dinner, we linger over the table.

4. He was an excellent wrestler, boxer, swimmer, and could play football well.

5. They marched through the fields, past a little village, and where there was a mountain path.

6. When I am well I like my daily swim, but in sickness I do not care for it.

7. We had to decide between two spots, Yeats's Thoor Ballylee or where he was buried.

8. For thirty years, in sunshine and when it rained, when it was cold and in the heat, Dan Murphy faithfully delivered the post.

9. He stole not only your property, but also I am missing my calculator.

10. The delegates from China, the Ambassadors from Brazil, and the American ambassadors were vetoed. (*Remember*, 'used in the same way'.)

11. Knowing how to study and to be able to budget time are important for college students.

12. The doctor recommended plenty of food, sleep, and to exercise regularly.

13. The ambassador from Sri Lanka spoke with warmth and humorously.

16. Apposition

Definition

Apposition is a general term rather than a specific structure. It means simply the placement of like grammatical structures next to each other. Any structure can be set in apposition so long as the writer observes the simple rule of parallel structure: join like grammatical items that function in the same way. Apposition allows a writer to add, modify, extend, deepen any phrase: noun phrases (the most common), prepositional phrases, adjective and adverb phrases. Because the appositive is a 'free' modifier, it is set off by commas as in the following examples.

Noun phrases

It seemed a new *idea*, a fresh *notion*, which cast new light where no one had yet looked. (*two objects*)

We ate at *Pierre's*, a new French *restaurant* beside the park. (*two objects*)

My *colleague*, an innovative *designer*, suggested that I should change my style. (*two subjects*)

Prepositional phrases

We found the information *in the stacks, in the poorly lit section* far to the back. (*two prepositional phrases*)

Adjective phrases

It was a *beautiful* sculpture, *sleek* and *inviting*.

Adverb phrases

The task was *well* done, *professionally*, *tastefully*.

Notice that the appositives themselves sometimes have further additions or modifiers. This enriches the modification, yet it is important to remember which key grammatical structures are being set in apposition, to remember to keep the structures parallel.

17. Correlative Conjunctions

Definition

Correlative Conjunctions are two-part coordinating conjunctions:

> not only . . . but also
> not only . . . but
> not . . . but
> either . . . or
> neither . . . nor
> both . . . and

All correlative conjunctions can be used to join either independent clauses or phrases within clauses. They are rhetorical devices. They give an emphasis to the parts they join: sometimes to both, sometimes just to the second one. It is important to watch in your writing that both parts of the correlative conjunction are parallel structures, that is like grammatical structures used in the same way: two subjects, two verbs, two objects, two clauses, etc.

Example 1 – JOINING TWO CLAUSES

Not only does this firm have an excellent track record but the competition looks to it for a performance standard.

Example 2 – JOINING TWO SUBJECTS

Both my friends and I feel that the rule is unfair.

Example 3 – JOINING TWO VERBS

You *either accept* the proposal the way it is worded *or reject* it altogether.

Example 4 – JOINING TWO OBJECTS

> They wanted to know **neither** our *excuses* **nor** our piteous *circumstances*.

Example 5 – JOINING TWO VERBAL PHRASES

> **Not** *thinking* ahead **but** *acting* on impulse, Gerald burst into the dark room and spoiled the negatives.

Example 6 – JOINING TWO PREPOSITIONAL PHRASES

> The increase in profit stemmed **not only** *from good marketing* **but also** *from efficient production*.

18. Punctuation[35]

. Full stop or Period

1. The full stop marks the end of a 'declarative' sentence.

2. Traditionally a full stop follows abbreviations:

   Misc.   Gen.   a.m.   Thurs.   no.

3. They are omitted from common abbreviations which are contractions (*where the abbreviation contains the first and last letter of the word*):

   Mr   Mrs   Dr

   from abbreviations in capital letters:

   RTÉ   BBC   BMW   IBM

   from acronyms that are pronounced as a word:

   DART   UNESCO   UNICEF   NASA

4. If an abbreviation comes at the end of a sentence, one full stop satisfies two needs.

   They packed everything they needed for the dig: picks, shovels, string, stakes, drawing pads, etc.

5. An ellipsis (which indicates an omission) in the middle of a sentence requires three full stops.

   The prolonged, arctic weather stream . . . brought heavy losses to farmers.

6. An ellipsis at the end of the sentence requires the three full stops plus a fourth, final one.

The prolonged, arctic weather stream, which poured
devastation upon all of Northern Europe, brought
heavy losses to farmers, to homeowners, to the
tourist industry. . . .

; Semicolon

1. The semicolon is sometimes called a weak full stop because it
    has a dual role – it joins as much as it separates elements. Like
    a full stop, it separates independent clauses. Yet it also
    juxtaposes two closely related ideas and implies that they are
    logically connected. It is nearly interchangeable with the
    coordinating conjunctions.

    Study these options:

    The tutor offered to negotiate the reading list.
    Everyone felt satisfied with the result. (*uses a full-stop*)

    The tutor offered to negotiate the reading list, so
    everyone felt satisfied with the result. (*shows cause-effect*)

    The tutor offered to negotiate the reading list, and
    everyone felt satisfied with the result. (*shows addition*)

    The tutor offered to negotiate the reading list;
    everyone felt satisfied with the result.
    (*unites by juxtaposition*)

    Notice that 'everyone' is not capitalised. Notice too the eco-
    nomical quality that the semicolon gives to the sentence.

2. The semicolon can also separate items in a series when each
    item is an extended phrase.

    The chef always insisted upon using the freshest
    meats, butchered that morning; organic vegetables
    and fruits that were vine or tree-ripened; and virgin
    olive oil, cold-pressed and imported from Italy.

, Comma

A rule of thumb about using commas: when in doubt, don't. In other words, the comma is not a breathing device. Its function is to mark the finish of one structure and the start of the next.

1. For instance, since a subordinating conjunction comes always at the beginning of a dependent clause, a comma will tell the reader where an initial dependent clause ends and the independent clause begins. The sentence you just read is an example.

2. Furthermore, the comma marks off introductory verbal phrases, items in a list, transition words, 'free' adjective clauses, and generally items set in apposition.

3. Where commas are used to separate items in a list, the inclusion of a comma before 'and' at the end of the list is optional:

    > The following students will be given extra work: Simms, O'Donovan, Jones, and Burke. (or Simms, O'Donovan, Jones and Burke.)

    It is helpful to include a comma at the end of a list or sequence when the final item includes 'and':

    > We enjoy looking at old movies, especially those with Marilyn Monroe, Laurel and Hardy, and Astaire and Rogers.

: Colon

The colon marks the place where an independent clause ends and either a list, a pronouncement, or a formal quotation starts. The colon gives emphasis, even drama, to any statement that follows it. Use it sparingly and it will retain its effect.

> I have one last sentiment to express: my gratitude.

> You will need three items of outer protection: gloves, a hat, and goggles.

> The chairman addressed the committee: 'This plenary session is concluded.'

−   Dashes
( )   Brackets or parentheses

Both allow a writer to insert information which is not part of the sentence structure.

> There were too many mysteries − soiled slippers, a bent key, freshly broken shrubbery − for the investigator to accept her story.

> The studies which corroborated his findings (O'Hanlon, 1995; Byrne, 1993) had long been accepted within the academic community.

The information inside the dashes and the brackets can be ignored and the sentences remain structurally intact. In my sense of the distinction between the two punctuation marks, the dash lends swiftness to a sentence; it speeds the reader along. The brackets interrupt the sentence and compel the reader either to linger or skip over the inclusion. Also, the brackets enclose material that could be put in a footnote.

A dash may also be used singly to indicate a hesitation in speech or an explanation:

> 'I thought I could go to − ' she said hesitatingly.

> 'Go where?' he replied.

> She was struck by the beauty of the landscape before her − mountains, trees, rivers.

> Mary could forget every mistake but the last − the destruction of her manuscript.

' '
" "   Quotation marks

1.   Direct speech: single quotation marks (inverted commas):

> He asked, 'How often have you looked for the book?'

2.   Punctuation which belongs to the quotation is place inside the mark; otherwise, it is placed outside the mark:

> She called out, 'We'll miss you!'.
> She called the baby 'a little doll'.
> Did I hear you say 'take that!'?

3. Single quotation marks surround cited words and phrases:

    Here is an example of 'poetic licence'.

4. Double vs Single quotation marks:

    Single marks surround a first quotation or citation; then double marks surround a quotation within a quotation or a citation within a quotation.

    > Several people called out, 'Is this an example of "poetic licence"?'

5. Single quotation marks surround titles of poems, stories, essays, and articles. Titles of all books, magazines, journals, reports, films, musical compositions, plays are italicised.

' Apostrophe

1. A plural noun does not take an apostrophe.

    the trees = more than one tree

    the libraries = more than one library

2. Both singular and plural possessive nouns require apostrophes. The placement of the apostrophe in relation to the 's' depends upon whether the noun is singular or plural.

    the library's location (*between the last letter and the s*)

    the libraries' system (*just following the final s*)

    Note: To nearly all proper nouns that end in s, we add an 's to the final s.

    Jesus's   Keats's   Dickens's   Yeats's   Giddens's

3. Plural nouns that do not end in s require 's.

    men's hats   women's thoughts   children's toys

4. A contraction is marked by an apostrophe.

    isn't = is not   I'd = I would/I had   hasn't = has not

    there's = there is   they're = they are

    it's = it is   he's = he is   she's = she is

Note: Problems arise around the verb 'is'. Notice the differences:

it's = it is   its = possessive of singular 'it'

who's = who is   whose = possessive of who
                             (like 'its', a possessive pronoun)

the apple's red = the apple is red

the apple's red [skin] = the apple possesses redness

it's red = it is red

its red [skin] = it has redness

The forms which most frequently give trouble to people are 'it's' and 'its'.

Footnote format

A generally accepted footnote system presents a citation in this manner:

> Declan Kiberd, *Inventing Ireland*, London, Jonathan Cape, 1995, p.286.
>
> Adele M. Dalsimer, 'Preface', *Kate O'Brien, A Critical Study*, Dublin, Gill & Macmillan, 1990, p. xi.
>
> Mary Cawley, 'Ireland: Habitat, Culture and Personality', in T. Bartlett, C. Curtin, R. O'Dwyer, G. Ó Tuathaigh (eds), *Irish Studies: A General Introduction*, Dublin, Gill & Macmillan, 1988, p.7.
>
> Stephen Mennell, 'Decivilising Processes: Theoretical Significance and Some Lines for Research', *International Sociology*, 5 (2), 1990, p.205-23.
> [*5 refers to the journal volume number and (2) refers to the issue published that year.*]

Bibliography Format

In a bibliography the above citations would change in two significant ways: (1) the surname comes first in a bibliography and is followed by a comma; (2) the date of publication comes after the author's name (in brackets). Thus, in a bibliography the citations above would appear in the following way (and in alphabetical order):

Cawley, Mary (1988) 'Ireland: Habitat, Culture and Personality', in T. Bartlett, C. Curtin, R. O'Dwyer, G. Ó Tuathaigh (eds), *Irish Studies: A General Introduction*, Dublin, Gill & Macmillan.

Dalsimer, Adele M. (1990) 'Preface', *Kate O'Brien, A Critical Study*, Dublin, Gill & Macmillan.

Kiberd, Declan (1995) *Inventing Ireland*, London, Jonathan Cape.

Mennell, Stephen (1990) 'Decivilising Processes: Theoretical Significance and Some Lines for Research', *International Sociology*, 5 (2).

19. Writing a Summary

Definition

A summary is a concise restatement, in your own words, of another, longer document, usually an article or a report. While a good working summary is written in your own words, you will want to borrow key phrases from the original.

Characteristics of a summary

(a) Above all, it must communicate the *meaning* of the original.
(b) It must adhere to the *facts* of the original.
(c) It must contain *all the main points* of the original.
(d) Usually it will not contain the supporting points, unless one or more of them is of unusual importance.
(e) It must *not contain your opinions* or views on the original.

Function

A good working summary should answer these questions:

(a) What is the *subject* of the original? What problem or situation is the writer addressing? (You might want to set this off as a separate paragraph, like an introduction, to make it stand out.)
(b) What are the *main points* of the original? The summary may or may not stick to the same order as the original. Normally summaries will cover the most important points first, although articles and reports often do not do that. If the original discusses some pro/con issue or compares two things, the summary will often give all the pro points together and all the con points together or keep the similar types of points together, even

though the original might not be organised that way. (If the original covers many main points, you might want to set them in separate paragraphs for clarity's sake.)

(c) What *conclusions* and *recommendations* does the original reach?

Steps in Writing a Summary

1. Read the original to get an overview of the whole piece. On a piece of rough paper, write in your own words the essential *point* of the piece, which you will likely find in the introduction, and its conclusion.

2. Reread and highlight the *important* ideas. Carefully check the beginnings of paragraphs for topic sentences that announce main points. Normally, you will not highlight supporting facts, but some may be so important that you will want to include them in your summary.

3. Now write the introductory statement of your summary, explaining what the original is about. Try to compose no more than two sentences.

4. Decide on the order you will present the main points of the original; on scratch paper try more than one order. Review the materials you have highlighted to make sure you cover everything.

5. Write the body of your summary, *using your own words* and making sure to cover all the key points.

6. Write your last part, in which you explain what the original author's conclusions were. Be sure to keep your own opinions out.

7. Proof-read for spelling, typographical errors, and the conventions of usage. In particular, compare the spelling of titles, authors, and other names and key terms with those in the original document.

20. Writing a Report

This chapter about report writing does several different things. First, it demonstrates how a report might look, being laid out as one. It defines a report and, in a list, says a little about each kind. Then it outlines the process one uses to prepare a report before formal writing begins. The preparation includes clarifying the terms of reference – the purpose and result – defining the reader, knowing how to separate different types of information, deciding upon an order according to the type of report it is – descriptive, analytical, persuasive, etc. In presenting the process of writing a report, the chapter touches upon ways one gathers information for the main body and briefly addresses conclusions and recommendations. There are exercises throughout and a checklist at the end.

Table of Contents

1.0 Introduction

1.1 Definition: A report is an ordered, logical statement which presents the facts about a situation or problem.

1.2 It may:

- simply record a sequence of events.
- interpret a set of particular facts.
- consider the case for and against a proposed course of action.
- discuss the likely effects of a decision or course of action.
- describe and evaluate the results of work or research.

1.3 It will:

- have a brief summary at the beginning, which is followed by an introduction of the terms of reference and the subject of the report.
- be divided under sectional headings and sub-headings.
- contain supporting evidence and illustrative material, some in the body, some in appendices.
- draw conclusions and may make recommendations.

1.4 There are many kinds of reports which range from informal to formal:

- The office memo is really an informal Letter report.
- The formal letter report should be constructed as a business letter and be written as tersely as possible. Here items might be numbered in a list as though the letter is a table of contents or cover letter which introduces something larger that follows and briefs the reader about what to expect.
- The minutes of a meeting enumerate the items in the meeting. They often contain an 'action by' column that apportions responsibility for certain tasks. The responsible person's name is set just beside the reported item.
- The purely descriptive information report can deal with the working of a single machine or can cover the operation of a large factory.

- The construction report shows actual and projected progress and costs, justifies existing methods of work, and suggests improvements. It may extend into periodic brief progress reports.

- A non-technical report, just as the non-technical summary or 'executive summary' within a report, informs a reader about a subject without using technical language. This is an exercise in translating one language into another.

- A preliminary report makes sound judgements before a project can be undertaken. It places great responsibility upon the writer.

- There are design reports, feasibility reports, reports on failures, and research reports.

- There is even the discussion report, meant for a professional meeting, a report which makes no conclusion but which sets the meeting's parameter and provides information to guide discussion.

1.5 Since the content of each report determines its precise structure, I will offer a generic and adaptable outline of a report's shape.

2.0 First Principles: Preparatory Considerations

Preparatory considerations are a pre-writing activity; they occur before actual composing of the text. Each of these preparatory points re-emerges during composition; therefore, certain points that I make in the preliminary considerations I will repeat when I address the layout of the report text.

2.1 Initially the writer must:

- Clarify terms of reference and need for the report
- Analyse the readership
- Have a system to collect information
- Have a system to store information.

2.2 Practical writing demands that the writer shall define the subject and the purpose of the report from the first moment. These are terms of reference, which also include information about who has requested the report. This definition begins to appear in the title and subtitle and is developed in the introductory statement, which predicts and steers the entire report. (See 6.4)

2.3 A second consideration at the initial stage of report writing is the reader. Who is the reader? What does the reader know about the subject? A writer is always better oriented when the reader is clearly defined.

- Is the reader a client who knows the technical language of the report or not? The answer to this single question will determine the balance the writer needs to find between explanatory and technical language.

- Is the reader a superior, a tutor, a supervisor? The answer will determine the level of formality in the report.

- Is the reader a colleague? If so, a technical shorthand will suffice, limiting the need for explanation and making the report more succinct.

- Does the writer know any of reader's opinions about the subject of the report?

- Is the reader possibly a speaker of another language?

- Is the readership international?

2.4 Exercise: the reader

An immediate superior has just joined your company and asked you for a report on your duties at work.

1. To define the reader, consider the attributes below.

2. Then write a brief statement of duties with your reader in mind. If you have no actual position from which to write, fabricate a position and write from it.

- Who is the primary reader?

- What does the reader know about the subject already?

- Does the reader have any known opinions or assumptions about the subject?

- Are there any secondary readers of the report?

- What does the reader need to know about the subject?

- Are there any special requirements or limitations on the report (perhaps it must be no longer than one page, or the reader lacks technical vocabulary, a deadline, the level of formality)? Define the limits before you write.
- What kind of response do you want to provoke in the reader?
- What future relationship (if any) will you have with the reader? Here the answer may be obvious, yet the question will have greater implications in other reports.

2.5 A third consideration is time. It must be taken as a first principle that time is limited and precious. One must be both brief and clear. Knowing the reader, a writer gives as much explanation as is needed for the sake of clarity and then moves on. And if a chart or picture says a thousand words, then a thousand words should be reduced to a caption. A reader will be able to detect that his or her time is being respected by the writer's economy and, therefore, will be more likely to stay with the report than if the writer's waffle, padding and cant parade about, taking up time. This is an issue of tact that shows, as well, the writer's control over the material.

3.0 Purpose

Having considered both reader and the scarcity of time, a writer must define the purpose of the report.

3.1 Is the report meant to persuade someone to buy, to select, or to do something? A writer selects the most compelling material and uses persuasive language. The negative aspects of a subject can be included as a sign of a writer's strong position. This inclusion indicates honesty and thoroughness. It also gives the writer an opportunity to show how the positive elements of the subject outnumber and outweigh the negative elements. The reader is left to decide, but the evidence is inescapable and the reader is persuaded.

3.2 Is the report meant to describe a structure, a process, a history of something (i.e. the workings of a factory or

one's projects over a given period)? If so, then a writer
logically arranges an order of presentation, initially as a
list, which best reflects the subject. This is an
organisational task largely. (See 7.0)

   3.2.1 In a descriptive report a writer may decide to
move in from an overview of a factory to a
close-up look at a particular item in it. Or
proceeding in the opposite direction, a writer
might begin focusing upon a particular item and
then move outward to encompass an overall
picture. Or the writer may decide to start at the
beginning of a process, let's say in manufacturing,
and follow it through to its end. Again, the
content dictates arrangement.

3.3 Is the report meant to synthesise a mass of information
from various sources: a collection of summaries, a file
of reports, a pile of research done by several people?
This requires assimilation and summarising. (See
chapter 19, Writing a Summary, pp. 137–8)

3.4 Is the report meant to judge a proposal, a project,
another report, or a situation for a civic body, for a
superior or colleagues? The approach should be balanced
and judicial as the writer presents several summary
aspects of the subject from various points of view.

4.0 Result (Object)

A writer's purpose in the report should be directed towards a
desired result in the reader.

- If the report's purpose is to persuade, the result should
be the reader's action or choice.

- If the report is descriptive, the reader will gain specific
knowledge of the topic, knowledge that might lead to a
further synthesis with other reports.

- If the report is itself a synthesis, the reader will acquire
knowledge or begin action or seek further synthesis.

- If the report makes a judgement, the reader may make
a decision.

4.1 Schema

Purpose	*Result/Object*
Persuade	Action; Choice
Describe	Knowledge
Synthesise	Action; Knowledge; Further synthesis
Judge	Decision

4.2 Exercise: persuasion leading towards a decision / choice

1. Choose an object (a calculator, software programme, some commodity, a proposal, etc.) and write two lists: one of positive features and one of negative features. This may include mention of a competitor's features.

2. Now order the items in each list from the most down to the least important.

3. Link those features from each list which relate to one another. (Simply draw a line.) You might use the positive side finally to determine your order of presentation.

4. Now write a page persuading your reader to choose your object.

4.3 Exercise: description leading to knowledge

Describe the daily operations of your office from the point of view of a client or customer.

1. How is your business used?

2. Make a list of functions and order them logically for use.

3. Perhaps guide the client through your operations along the lines of one particular need.

5.0 Preliminary Organisation

Once the first principles, the purpose, and its intended result are clearly defined, a report writer begins the preliminary organisation of the report. Even before starting formal composition, a writer begins actively gathering information, reading, note taking, writing down bits of text as threads begin to weave together. Initially active reading and writing go on together, but the writing is not formally organised. Formal sequence comes later.

5.1 Types of information

In researching and gathering materials for a report, a writer sorts and stores three kinds of information. The writer should set up a consistent system of storing this material: cards with headings, computer files, notebooks with sections.

5.1.1 **Mainstream information** relates directly to the topic of the report. This goes into the main body of the report.

5.1.2 Related **back-up information** goes into footnotes or appendices. The main body should not be cluttered with related tangential material because of the first principle of the scarcity of time. If it is organised under headings in an appendix, an interested reader can pursue it while the uninterested reader is spared wading through material of secondary importance in order to get to the essentials of the report.

5.1.3 **Interesting information** is discovered along the path of research yet is not related to the topic of the report at all. This can be filed away for future study.

5.2 Process

A writer jots down general categories as they emerge during the research. This is often a process of discovery. Under these category headings the writer places the related information. Some information will tend towards more than one category. It should be put into each one until later when it can be sorted accurately.

5.3 Order

A writer may be uncertain about the best order to place the categories in the report. This organisational question requires a step back for a little perspective. What is the report about?

- Does it describe a process? Then the categories might be put into the order of the construction of something or a logical sequence of time.
- Is the report persuasive or evaluative? Then the categories might best be placed in a hierarchy of importance.

- Is the report a synthesis. Then the categories might be organised to present an increasing complexity as the information forms layers and grows more dense. (See 7.0)

5.4 The categories will help the writer to form section headings, which should be numbered. From this general notation – best given in decimal numbers – paragraph numbering will follow. Thus

- Chapter heading: 1.0
- Subsection: 1.1
- Paragraph: 1.1.1

6.0 Layout

6.1 Layout

The layout of the report should include:

- Title
- Summary (purpose and results)
- Introduction (terms of reference: subject and purpose)
- Main Body (detail of purpose–method–results)
- Conclusions
- Recommendations

6.2 Title

The Title of the report indicates the topic of the report and is like a mini thesis statement. It is linked to the Introduction, which enlarges the title in the exposition of the subject, i.e., terms of reference.

6.3 Summary

To the reader who has little time, the Summary offers the fruit of the report. It is a succinct statement of objectives, of important findings and of any conclusions and recommendations the report has finally reached. Here a writer articulates the essence of the report by presenting only the important points. The reader might go no further than the summary. Therefore, it is a crucial part of the report. This is sometimes called an 'executive summary'. (See chapter 19, Writing a Summary, pp. 137–8.)

6.4 Introduction

The Introduction section of the report first states the terms of reference, states, that is, why the report is being written and what it is primarily about. It states the report's matter under investigation, its purpose, scope, and result. If the report has been requested, the terms of reference identify who has made the request. If the writer produces the report by his or her own initiative, s/he tells the purpose in doing so. In sum, the terms of reference charge the writer to:

- investigate a defined subject for a specifically stated purpose;

- conduct the investigation within clearly stated parameters;

- formulate conclusions and recommendations, even though what these are cannot be stated fully in the terms of reference.

6.4.1 Introduction examples

- TERMS OF REFERENCE

The terms of reference authorised by the Managing Director for this report are as follows:

1. to investigate the current delays in production of compact disc cleaner kits;

2. to examine alternative methods of overcoming the delays;

3. to make recommendations, accordingly.

- TERMS OF REFERENCE

On 23 May 1998, the General Manager requested the members of the Works Council to investigate the services provided by the Works Canteen, report on their findings and make any necessary recommendations.

• LETTER FORMAT

All Downhill, Ltd.
Plumbers
543 Fen Rd.
Drainage, Co. Trappe
Tel: 09-876543

15 August 1998

Mr T.R. Watershed
Hawthorne Cottage
Bramblebush

Dear Mr Waterford,

Mains Water Supply

You instructed me on 30 May 1998 to
investigate the potential for obtaining a mains
water connection to your cottage, and authorised
me to consult with Trappe Water on your behalf.
I have now discussed the matter with their Area
Engineer and . . .

6.4.2 Introduction exercise: establishing terms of reference

• First, think of a problem in your place of
  work which, for the sake of this exercise,
  merits investigation and a report. It could be
  a problem in organisation, communication,
  production, morale, car parking, telephone
  use, photocopying, coffee room.
• Second, think of an appropriate title and write
  the terms of reference for your report.

6.5 Second requirement

Second in the introduction, a writer formally introduces
the subject (topic) or thesis of the report in an
expository statement. This is the opening statement to
which every paragraph in the report's main body is
somehow linked. It is useful to write a draft of this
statement early in the process as it clarifies and guides

the writing. A writer can return to the thesis statement and modify it as new information dictates, until in the end it is both a complete and succinct statement of the subject. Pin it to the wall next to your desk; look at it frequently.

6.6 Third requirement

Third in the introduction, a writer

- explains the approach and special terms used in the report,

- tells how the information was gathered (in the field, by correspondence, in a research library, by experiment),

- and tells how it is presented in text, charts, photos, etc.

This orients the reader's expectations and instructs him or her in how to read the report.

6.7 Fourth requirement

A writer must clarify the limitations which are imposed upon the report, so the fourth requirement is that the reader is told what has been left out. If it is a report on the impeller water pump, for instance, the writer needs to state that it ignores the syphon pump and other designs. This negative definition again helps to form the reader's expectations.

6.8 Final requirement

Finally in the introduction, a writer cites the sources of information.

7.0 Main Body of the Report

The main body of the report must contain facts and nothing but facts. This is no place for a writer's personal opinions, inferences, prejudices, or even recommendations. These modes of the report come later in the conclusion and recommendation. The main body is reserved for a presentation of data.

7.1 Gathering the data

- by interview
- by study of paperwork
- by observation of operations, procedures
- by inspection of sites, locations

Vital to each of the above:

- an examination and analysis of the facts and data. By analysis, I mean an exposition of constituent parts contained in the data. This is not interpretation or inference.

7.1.1 By interview

Remember the interviewer's questions:

who? what? where? when? why? how?

While a report writer keeps opinions out of this portion of the report, he or she must include the views of the interviewee *precisely* as they are stated.

7.1.2 By study of paperwork

A writer must follow all paper trails (circulation routes, addressees, cross references, back up files, etc.) since information that is absent in one location will probably turn up in a different place. A writer pursues all leads and at least glances at every scrap of information that is even slightly related to the subject. A writer should gather more information than he or she needs to write the report. (See 5.1)

7.1.3 By observation of procedures in site inspections

During a site inspection, a writer should have a note pad, camera, tape recorder, a tape measure, a calculator, and a list of items to inspect.

7.1.3.1 Checklist for a progress report or accident report

- Make adequate photographic coverage. If it is a progress report (i.e. construction), try to get before as well as after pictures.

- Draw a scaled plan of the area, depicting all relevant detail.

- By eye-witness, observation, and any physical evidence, establish the extent and nature of any progress or delays (progress report) or any consequences in the sequence of events (accident report) that you can.

- Get written statements from those you have interviewed officially, and check each interviewee's future availability in case you need to interview that person further.

7.2 Organising the data

On one hand, subject matter dictates the logical order of presentation of the categories, which are neat, digestible pieces. On the other hand, the type of report – persuasion, description, narration, exposition, synthesis, judgement – also determines the order of presentation. Of course, these modes are mixed in most reports. Still, one will dominate and determine the report's general organisation and tone.

7.2.1 The **argument** or **persuasion** type of report advances a case for something, or against something. Using the facts, a writer discusses the value of a subject, discusses its features, gathers informed opinions and works towards a conclusion and recommendation. Pro and con points must be organised in a consistent manner so that the reader does not get confused. A writer must keep personal opinion clearly distinct from fact and from the reported opinions of interviewees.

7.2.2 The **description type** of report forms a picture that the reader can imagine. A writer chooses words, phrases and statements which evoke colour, shape, size; it is a sensory construction. The most accurate adjectives help the reader to see the subject. A thesaurus broadens word choice, gives variety, and also helps a writer to avoid repetition.

7.2.3 The **narrative** type of report presents a sequence of events, usually in chronological order or in spatial movement from place to place. This narrative might follow the movement of an assembly line from beginning to end or recount the stages in a prolonged experiment.

7.2.4 The **exposition** type of report, like both description and narration, explains how something works, or it gives the facts about a situation, or makes some kind of claim. Taking its name from the same root as expository writing (the essay), it exposes something in logical order according to the nature of that subject. It proceeds by logical thinking, step by step from stage to stage. Much instructional material is expositive reporting. A writer must be careful not to omit a step which the reader might need to understand the relationship of one part of the material to another. Of course, this logic is true in all writing; therefore, this type touches all reports. Still, it is more objective than persuasive writing; the writer's judgement is less important.

7.2.5 The **synthesis** type of report uses the technique of summary. A writer brings together summaries of related reports, essays, experiments and research, and reports findings based upon the union, or synthesis, of all this research.

7.2.6 Here are various schemes for presenting material in logical order:

- **Chronological order**: It is best suited to narrative.

- Order of **ascending importance**: the main points come last. This is useful when a writer wants the main argument to be a culmination.

- Order of **descending importance**: the main points come first. This is useful when a writer wants the main point to have initial impact and then reinforces it with supporting points. This order puts the main point across to the impatient reader who is pressed for time.

- Order from the **general to the particular**. This order is useful when a writer describes a visit to some location. It starts with an overview and focuses in on particulars.

- Order from the **particular to the general**. This order helps a writer to make a general point which arises out of several specific examples. An accident report might work from the incident to a general safety problem on site.

- Order by **aspects of a subject**. This pattern in exposition helps a writer to break items into mentally digestible portions which are also logically, progressively staged.

7.2.7 Exercise: order of sentences in a paragraph

Take a paragraph you have written and write each sentence out on a small piece of paper. You can then move these pieces of paper about to see what the effect is of placing sentences in different positions. For instance, change a paragraph sequence from a general to specific progression to the reverse. (A similar exercise can be carried out with whole paragraphs within an essay.) You can discover better arrangements for your paragraphs this way. Or do the exercise with a complex sentence, one with an independent and dependent clause joined into one sentence. You can observe different ways of ordering the parts, of shifting emphasis, by introducing first one element, then trying another in its place.

7.2.8   Exercise: a mini-report

Write a mini-report on a subject for which you require little or no preparation – for instance, your current workload for a week's period. Make out a diary-report for the week ahead, breaking each day into 30-minute periods. See Layout, 6.1, for all the parts of a report and include them all.

8.0   Conclusion

A conclusion draws together threads of the report as a summary. It is a recapitulation and may well mirror the introductory statements in the non-technical or 'executive' summary. Now, however, the reader listens to the summation not with an expectation of what is to come but with a knowledge that the report has given. It is a look back, truly a recapitulation. A conclusion may clinch an argument, it may answer a question posed by the report, it may make its final persuasion. This can lead to a recommendation.

9.0   Recommendation

A recommendation extends beyond the conclusion in that it proposes steps which might be taken to improve problematic conditions that the report has described in detail. The recommendation might be the goal towards which an entire report points from its very beginning.

10.0   Review Checklist

Read through the report and check it for all the loose ends, from content to grammar. This check includes organisation, technical accuracy, semantics (word choice), as well as the structural elements such as syntax, grammar, punctuation and spelling. It is necessary to check the content and the structural aspects in two separate readings because it is impossible to monitor both closely at once; it is like trying to focus on foreground and background simultaneously. Here is a checklist that will help.

10.1 **Content checklist**

10.1.1 Overall organisation:

- Have you kept the reader in mind and written for him and her or for yourself?
- Is any section irrelevant, off the subject?
- Are all the data accurate?
- Have you overlooked any details?

10.1.2 Sentence level:

- Are your tenses uniform? Are tense changes deliberate? Do your subjects and verbs agree?
- Are the sentence structures correct?
- Are there any typographical errors? Errors in punctuation? Spelling?
- Is there any ambiguity in your statements or word choice?
- Does the report read smoothly, coherently; does it have the same voice throughout it? Is your idiom appropriate? Too formal, too informal?

10.1.3 Satisfied expectations:
- Does the title fit the contents of the report?
- Have you met the objectives? Have you fulfilled the terms of reference?
- Are your conclusions and recommendations clearly justified by the facts you have provided in the main body of the report?

10.2 **Structural checklist**

- Given your layout scheme, have you placed the sections in the best order? Is the layout consistent?
- Are there unnecessary repetitions of sections or within sections?
- Are you satisfied with your paragraph organisation?

- Are there any parts in the body of the report from which some information should be taken and put into an appendix?

10.2.1 Exercise

Select a report which you have written recently and analyse it using this checklist. Make a note of which items in the checklist you find most helpful. Are there any items you would add to the list?

Solutions to Exercises

Chapter 4

Exercise 2, p. 16
1–S, 2–S, 3–F, 4–F, 5–S, 6–F, 7–S, 8–F, 9–F, 10–F, 11–S, 12–F, 13–S

Chapter 7

Exercise 1, p. 43
1–and, 2–or, 3–nor, 4–but/yet, 5–and/yet, 6–for, 7–nor, 8–so

Exercise 2, p. 44
1–but/yet, 2–or, 3–for, 4–and, 5–so, 6–but/yet, 7–nor

Exercise 3, pp. 44–5
1–so, 2–yet/but, 3–but, 4–and/but, 5–so, 6–and, 7–but, 8–so/and,
9–nor, 10–for, 11–so, 12–for, 13–nor, 14–so/and, 15–but, 16–for,
17–or

Chapter 11

Exercise 1, p. 105
1–who, 2–whom, 3–whom, 4–who, 5–who, 6–who, 7–whom,
8–whom, 9–of whom, 10–who, 11–who, 12–whom, 13–who,
14–who, 15–whom, 16–who

Exercise 2, p. 106
1–that, 2–that, 3–where, 4–that, 5–which, 6–whom, 7–whose,
8–when, 9–beside which, 10–whom, 11–which, 12–whose,
13–when, 14–who, 15–when

Notes

1 I derive this scheme of paragraph study from Francis Christensen and Bonnijean Christensen, who developed it in 'The Generative Rhetoric of the Paragraph', *Notes Toward a New Rhetoric*, 2nd edition, New York, Harper & Row, 1978.

2 David Macaulay, *The Way Things Work*, Boston, Houghton Mifflin Co., 1988, p. 10.

3 Cathleen O'Neill, 'Censorship and the Arts', *Let in the Light: Censorship, Secrecy and Democracy*, Ellen Hazelkorn and Patrick Smyth, eds, Dingle, Brandon, 1993.

4 R.F. Foster, *Modern Ireland, 1600–1972*, London, Allen Lane, Penguin, 1988, p.6.

5 Gail Seekamp, *Personal Finance*, Dublin, Oak Tree Press, 1996, p. 4.

6 See H.W. Fowler, *A Dictionary of Modern English Usage*, 2nd edition, article on 'and' no. 5, Oxford, Oxford University Press, 1965, p. 29; or 3rd edition, R.W. Burchfield, ed., article on 'and' no. 3, Oxford, Clarendon Press, 1996, p. 52.

7 John J. Lynch and Frank W. Roche, *Business Management in Ireland*, Dublin, Oak Tree Press, 1995 p. xxiii.

8 Kenneth C. Slagle, 'Introduction' to Henry Mackenzie's *The Man of Feeling*, New York, W.W. Norton, 1958, p. v.

9 Adele M. Dalsimer, 'Preface', *Kate O'Brien, A Critical Study*, Dublin, Gill & Macmillan, 1990, p. xi.

10 E.B. White, 'Here is New York', *Essays of E.B.White*, New York, Harper & Row, 1977, p. 123.

11 Paul Johnson, 'From the Boer War to Berlin', review of Martin Gilbert's *A History of the 20th Century: Vol. 1 1900–1933*, in *The Sunday Times: Books*, 20 July 1997.

12 Bernice Grohskopf, 'The Treasure', *The Treasure of Sutton Hoo*, New York, Atheneum, 1973, p. 57.

13 Mark Tierney, 'The Debt Trap', *Consumer Choice,* July 1997.
14 Erich Auerbach , 'Odysseus' Scar', *Mimesis,* Princeton, Princeton University Press, 1946, 1973 edition, p. 3.
15 Lynch and Roche, *Business Management in Ireland,* p. 34.
16 Alistair Scott, from article on ski resorts, in 'Travel', *The Sunday Times,* 12 October 1997.
17 Mary Cawley, 'Ireland: Habitat, Culture and Personality', *Irish Studies: A General Introduction,* T. Bartlett, C. Curtin, R.O'Dwyer, and G.Ó Tuathaigh, eds, Dublin, Gill & Macmillan, 1988, p. 7.
18 Example taken from Robert Benson, 'Paragraph Modelling', *Sentence and Paragraph Modelling* by James Gray and Robert Benson, Berkeley, Bay Area Writing Project, Curriculum Publication No. 17, 1982, p. 36.
19 Seekamp, *Personal Finance,* p. 47.
20 Ibid., p. 47.
21 Lynch and Roche, *Business Management in Ireland,* p. 36.
22 Benson in Gray and Benson, *Sentence and Paragraph Modelling,* pp. 44–5.
23 Irma Rombauer, *The Joy of Cooking,* New York, Bobbs-Merrill, 1975, p. 599.
24 Paul Johnson in *The Sunday Times: Books,* 20 July 1997.
25 Augustine Martin, 'Introduction', *The Genius of Irish Prose,* A. Martin, ed., Cork, Mercier Press, 1985, p. 7.
26 Colbert Kearney, 'The Short Story: 1900–1945', *The Genius of Irish Prose,* A. Martin, ed., Cork, Mercier Press, 1985, p. 33.
27 Patrick Sheeran, 'The Irish Tradition and Nineteenth-Century Fiction: A Review', *Irish Studies: A General Introduction,* T. Bartlett, C. Curtin, R. O'Dwyer, and G. Ó Tuathaigh, eds, Dublin, Gill & Macmillan, 1988, p. 87.
28 Declan Kiberd, 'Inventing Irelands', *Inventing Ireland,* London, Jonathan Cape, 1995, p. 286.
29 Terence Brown, 'Decades of Debate', *Ireland: A Social and Cultural History, 1922–1985,* London, Fontana, 1981, 1990, p. 272.
30 Anthony Roche, *Contemporary Irish Drama,* Dublin, Gill & Macmillan, 1994, pp. 74–5.
31 Thomas Pakenham, 'Introduction', *Dublin, A Travellers' Companion,* New York, Atheneum, 1988, p. 27.
32 Forster, E.M., 'My Wood', *Abinger Harvest,* London, Harcourt Brace Jovanovich, 1936, 1964.
33 Joan Didion, 'Georgia O'Keeffe', *The White Album,* New York, Simon & Schuster, 1979.

34 Tom Boylan, Chris Curtin, Michael Laver, 'A Changing Society: Ireland Since the 1960s', *Irish Studies: A General Introduction,* T. Bartlett, C. Curtin, R. O'Dwyer, and G. Ó Tuathaigh, eds, Dublin, Gill & Macmillan, 1988, pp. 192–200.

35 I have consulted *The Concise Oxford Dictionary*, 9th edition, Appendix XIII, 'Style Guide, A. Punctuation Marks', Oxford, Oxford University Press, 1995.

Index